THE ULTIMATE GUIDE TO

D040190G

TRADING CARD GAMES

BY MICHAEL G. RYAN

DISCOVER SOME OF THE GREATEST TRADING CARD GAMES OF ALL TIME!

FOR YOUR PARENTS!

. . . .

Richard Garfield, PhD, created an entire industry when he invented the trading card game Magic: The Gathering® *in 1993. Hundreds of games have been released since with the same general concept: you use your cards, I'll use mine, and we'll play a game together. With two children of his own, Garfield has newfound perceptions of what's possible with trading card games.*

KIDS AND TRADING CARD GAMES

As long as I can remember, I've thought that games were underutilized in education. Every game I played in my youth seemed to have educational potential, from teaching simple facts—like the countries in *Risk*®—to thinking abstractly, as in chess. As I grew older, I saw social lessons taught in multiplayer games like *Diplomacy*®, and lessons about probability taught in card and dice games.

As my children have grown up, I have tried to encourage them to love games. When we began, I remember them working to count the pips on a die. Then I saw how each time we played it became more automatic. I took pleasure as they got closer to beating me in simple memory games and pleasure in their eventual victories. Now that they are eight and ten years old, we deal with more sophisticated games. We talk about probabilities and strategies, and we enjoy finding reflections of a game's dynamics in real life.

Trading card games have added something special: the notion that not all players need to have the same equipment. In life, people have different resources, so it's easy to imagine how participating in a game structured this way could bring different lessons to the table.

With trading card games, the act of trading and collecting cards teaches far more about economics than a game previously could. With traditional games, someone owns the game, and so all the economy is "within" the game. With the distributed structure of trading card games, players are participating in a very real economic system. Cards fluctuate in value as players discover new strategies. When players don't value things in the same way, you learn that there are many opportunities for trade that leave all parties happy. This lesson is frequently lost in a traditional closed-environment zero-sum game.

Players can develop a sense of wonder and discovery through a game that feels endless. In traditional games, players seeking mastery get complete understanding of the big things and focus harder on minutia. The games then pivot on the mastery of this information. Trading card games, however, are more like life, where the big picture changes often enough that minutia can stay minutia.

But mastering this endless minutia in trading card games can be satisfying for a kid. Probably the second most common comment I get from parents is about how much children who are interested in a trading card game show improved reading skills. These kids are given a vast set of information that is of great interest to them, and it's only accessible through reading.

The MOST common comment I get is that trading card games have given the parents something interactive and fun to do with their child during the journey through adolescence. As a child grows, the rules that govern their relationships with their family, friends, teachers, and institutions all change. Having games as a common bond gives one an anchor point, a place where the rules are understood and stable. At the same time, exploring the ever-changing realm of a trading card game allows exploration of new rules in a safe, understood manner. I believe this bond not only provides comfort but also provides tools that could be valuable throughout life.

So, if your child is interested in trading card games, consider exploring the world with them. And if this doesn't turn out to interest you, invite them into the world of the games you grew up with that *do* interest you. Kids are usually delighted to be part of more than one world . . . something we could all learn from!

FOR YOU!

DISCOVER A NEW WORLD!

Trading card games have only been around since 1993, when Richard Garfield invented *Magic: The Gathering*. This might seem like a long time to you if you're only ten years old, but think about this: video games have been around since 1972, *Monopoly*® was invented in 1935, and chess has been a popular game for almost 1,500 years, a thousand times longer than trading card games!

And trading card games get more popular every year for a lot of different reasons. Here are five reasons why so many kids are playing games like Pokémon, Bella Sara, Naruto, Yu-Gi-Oh!, and Bakugan Battle Brawlers:

1. They're easy to learn! With a rulebook or with a friend, you can be ready to play in no time.

2. They're fun to collect and trade—and every time you add new cards to your collection, you might discover a new way to play the cards you already have.

3. They teach you all kinds of things, like reading, math, and new ways to think about problems and how to solve them.

4. They're a great way to make new friends. Many local libraries, community centers, and game stores host events where you can make new friends who are as excited about the game as you are. Together, you can play the game and test your skills.

5. They're rewarding! You can enter a league and win prizes, go online and collect points, or even compete to be one of the top-ranked players in the country . . . or the world!

TOP CARDS FOR EACH GAME!

The lists in this book might not be the top cards for everyone, but they'll definitely show you some of the best cards in each game. So, try your favorite or try them all. A whole new world is waiting for you when you open your first pack of trading cards, and you're going to have a great time exploring that world!

TRAINERS: WELCOME TO THE WORLD OF THE POKÉMON TRADING CARD GAME!

Gotta catch 'em all! The Pokémon phenomenon started in Japan in 1996, and it took the United States by storm two years later. It hasn't slowed down since! More than 490 different Pokémon—each with its own power, type, strengths, and weaknesses—have been introduced since the game began. Players (called Trainers) catch, raise, and do battle against other Trainers using the many different Pokémon they have collected. The goal: to become a Pokémon Master!

Each year, four new sets of cards, called expansions, are released for players to add to their collections and to the decks they build for battle. These battles are easy to find; lots of local stores support leagues through Pokémon Organized Play. For the more experienced players, there are premier events like city or state championships. For those who truly want to become a Pokémon Master, there's the ultimate battle—the World Championships!

All you need to get started is a theme deck and a friend. After that, you can decide which Pokémon you like best and start building a deck of your own.

From the cute Pokémon like Pikachu and Piplup to the fearsome and powerful Pokémon like Charizard and Darkrai, the Pokémon Trading Card Game has exciting Pokémon for Trainers of all ages to catch and train. Who knows? You might be the next Pokémon Master!

LET'S PLAY!

In the Pokémon Trading Card Game, you and your opponent each have a deck of 60 cards. Each deck contains all the Pokémon, Energy cards, and Trainer cards you need to battle.

You will set some cards aside as Prize cards; these will be your rewards when you Knock Out your opponent's Pokémon in battle.

After you each draw cards, you'll place some Basic Pokémon facedown as your Active Pokémon (the one you'll fight with first) and as your Benched Pokémon (the ones that are waiting to join the battle later). You'll turn them over when it's time to play.

On your turn, you'll attach an Energy card to your Pokémon so they can use their attacks, you'll play Trainer cards that will help you in battle, you'll evolve your Pokémon (by putting Stage 1 Pokémon on your Basic Pokémon, or by putting Stage 2 Pokémon on your Stage 1 Pokémon), and you'll use their Poké-Bodies and Poké-Powers to get ready. And, finally, you'll battle your opponent's Pokémon!

Sometimes you'll figure out how the battle goes by looking at Weakness and Resistance on the battling Pokémon. You'll put damage counters on each Pokémon to show how the fight went, and you'll check each Pokémon's Hit Points (HP) to see who won. Sometimes you might want to change the Active Pokémon you were going to fight with for one on your Bench, so you'll retreat.

And in the end, one of you might Knock Out the other player's Pokémon and draw a Prize card.

When you draw your last Prize card, you win!

To get started, try out a Trainer Kit—it'll give you all you need to start on the path of becoming a Pokémon Master!

NAME: Wailord

SET: *Diamond & Pearl–Great Encounters* (2008)

#25

IT'S COOL BECAUSE: Wailord is a fantastic wall—with 200 HP (the most of any Pokémon in the entire history of the game), it can hold off your opponent's attacks for a long time while you build up other Pokémon on your Bench. Plus, if you're able to combine its attack with its Poké-Body, you might be removing damage counters from it between turns, making your Wailord wall last longer!

COMBO PLATTER!

Try Wailord with Potion, Pokémon Night Center, Leftovers, or Dawn Stadium to take off those damage counters even faster!

NAME: Rare Candy
SET: *Diamond & Pearl–Great Encounters* (2008)

IT'S COOL BECAUSE: Rare Candy isn't even a rare card, but it's popular because it's so useful. It's the fastest way to get your basic Charmander evolved to your Stage 2 Charizard. It works even better if you use it with other Pokémon or Trainer cards that let you search your deck for Pokémon. Many of the best decks in the world use this Trainer card to get rare, powerful Pokémon into play on the very first turn!

IN ANY OTHER LANGUAGE . . .

The Pokémon Trading Card Game is available in many different languages—French, German, Italian, Portuguese, Spanish, Japanese, and English. Some of the terms in the game are easy to recognize in other languages ("Resistenz" in German, "Benchi" in Japanese, and "Carta Energia" in Italian). Here's a harder one: what do you think the English game term is for this word?

French: Faiblesse
German: Schwäche
Italian: Debolezza

Japanese: Jyakuten
Portuguese: Fraqueza
Spanish: Debilidad

Answer: *Weakness*

NAME: Mesprit LV.X
SET: *Diamond & Pearl–Legends Awakened* (2008)

IT'S COOL BECAUSE: This is the most recent hot card to join the cool list. It's a LV.X card, which are among the most powerful cards available! Mesprit LV.X has an okay attack in Supreme Blast (it's a little hard to get all those LV.X cards in play to make it work), but it has a really great attack in Healing Look: you could remove as many as 15 damage counters from your Benched Pokémon every turn . . . for free!

FAST COMBO!

Use Premier Ball from *Great Encounters* to ensure that you get Mesprit LV.X (or Uxie LV.X and Azelf LV.X, so you can use Mesprit's Supreme Blast) into your hand as fast as possible!

NAME: Blaziken ex

SET: *EX Team Magma vs Team Aqua* (2004)

. . . .

IT'S COOL BECAUSE: This card looked way too powerful to many players when it came out—its first attack looked strong, but its second attack looked like it would break the whole game! It has a cheap attack, does a lot of damage, and when you use it with other cards that let you move Energy around, it seems unstoppable. Many powerful decks were built around this card, including a second-place deck at the 2004 World Championships!

Blaziken ex — 150 HP

STAGE 2 — Evolves from Combusken

When Pokémon-ex has been Knocked Out, your opponent takes 2 Prize cards.

Illus. Hikaru Koike

Blaze Kick — 30+

Flip a coin. If heads, this attack does 30 damage plus 20 more damage. If tails, this attack does 30 damage and the Defending Pokémon is now Burned.

Volcanic Ash

Discard 2 Energy attached to Blaziken ex and then choose 1 of your opponent's Pokémon. This attack does 100 damage to that Pokémon. *(Don't apply Weakness and Resistance for Benched Pokémon.)*

weakness — resistance — retreat cost

©2004 Pokémon/Nintendo

IN A LEAGUE OF ITS OWN

Pokémon Trainers have some great opportunities to challenge others through Pokémon Organized Play. Leagues can connect you to stores, libraries, or community centers in your area where other players bring their decks and test their skills. Sometimes you can earn prizes along the way. You can also get in on tournaments, Championship events, and sneak-preview Prereleases by becoming part of the Pokémon TCG community.

You can learn lots more about Pokémon Organized Play and all the events it supports by checking it out, with your parent's permission, at the official Pokémon Web site!

#21

NAME: Empoleon LV.*X*
SET: *Diamond & Pearl* (2007)

IT'S COOL BECAUSE: Fans were extremely excited to get their hands on the three first-ever LV.*X* cards when *Diamond & Pearl* finally came out. Piplup, Chimchar, and Turtwig were already easy to recognize, and their super-powerful LV.*X* cards were very popular with the collectors. Though Empoleon from *Majestic Dawn* has better attacks, Empoleon LV.*X* is still a fan favorite!

MISS THE MISTAKE?

When it was first released, Empoleon LV.*X* from the *Diamond & Pearl* expansion had a pretty noticeable mistake on the card— do you see it?

Answer: Instead of the words "Poké-Power" in red text, it had the words "Poké-Body" in green text. This might have caused rules problems, so the card was quickly fixed, but the version with the mistake became a collector's piece!

#20

NAME: Birthday Pikachu
SET: Promo card (2000)

IT'S COOL BECAUSE:
Though you can't play the card in any official games (because it's too easy for anyone to claim it's their birthday!), this is still an unusual card to have because of the fill-in-the-blank parts of the card. It's the only one like that in the whole game. Plus, every time someone fills in one of those blanks, there's one less perfect Birthday Pikachu card out there to collect, making all the rest of them even more valuable!

Basic Pokémon

's Pikachu 50 HP

Mouse Pokémon. Length: 1' 4", Weight: 13 lbs.

Birthday Surprise If it's not your birthday, this attack does 30 damage. If it is your birthday, flip a coin. If heads, this attack does 30 damage plus 50 more damage; if tails, this attack does 30 damage.

30+

weakness   resistance   retreat cost

Your Birthdate: _____   LV. 17 #25

Illus. Kagemaru Himeno   ©1995, 96, 98 Nintendo, Creatures, GAMEFREAK, ©1999-2000 Wizards   24

POP QUIZ!

Pokémon have been featured on the cover of which famous U.S. magazines?

    A) *TV Guide* and *Time*

    B) *Newsweek* and *Rolling Stone*

    C) *Entertainment Weekly* and *People*

Answer: A) Both magazines featured multiple Pokémon in late 1999.

NAME: Venusaur ex
SET: *FireRed & LeafGreen* (2004)

IT'S COOL BECAUSE: Venusaur is a more powerful version by being a Pokémon-ex. It has some problems, such as two Weaknesses and an expensive Retreat Cost. But since it can move as much Grass Energy as it likes each turn, you can build it up fast to do that powerful Solarbeam attack. And if it looks like Venusaur ex's impressive150 HP won't save it, you can move all the Grass Energy off of it before it gets Knocked Out! Plus, its Pollen Hazard attack is probably going to give your opponent's Pokémon all sorts of trouble.

PLAY LIKE A CHAMPION!

Imagine how difficult it must be to create a World Championship-winning deck. Well, you don't have to figure it out on your own because every year after the Pokémon TCG World Championships, the four best decks of the year are released for you to try out for yourself! They are available for a limited time each fall. With special backs and borders, these decks are exactly like the ones the Champions won their titles with. They're great for learning inside secrets and card combinations to help you build your own powerful decks in the future!

NAME: Claydol
SET: *Diamond & Pearl–Great Encounters* (2008)

#18

IT'S COOL BECAUSE: In the 2008 National Championships, nearly 66% of all the decks had Claydol in them. Why? Because it lets you go through your deck at an amazing speed, finding all those other super-cool cards you need in order to win. Even better, it can do it from your Bench, so you can have two or three Claydol letting you race through every card in your deck!

WORD TO THE WISE!

Claydol lets you draw cards only if you have fewer than six cards in your hand, so don't put other popular card-drawing cards, like Steven's Advice, in your deck. You won't need them once you have a Claydol or two in play!

#17

#16

#15

NAMES: Call Energy/Scramble Energy/Double Rainbow Energy

SETS: *Diamond & Pearl–Majestic Dawn* (2008)
EX Dragon Frontiers (2006)
EX Crystal Guardians (2006)

THEY'RE COOL BECAUSE: Energy cards may not seem exciting at first, but the best players know that you need to use *every* opportunity in the game to increase the power of your deck. Call Energy gets you inside your deck quickly so you can get access to your Basic Pokémon. If you know you're going to have evolved Pokémon in your deck, both Double Rainbow Energy and Scramble Energy are sure things. They both give quick boosts to the Pokémon they're attached to. And since they can be any kind of Energy you need, they can be attached to any Pokémon you like!

DECK-BUILDING ADVICE

You're allowed to have four of each Special Energy card in your deck. Practice with different amounts of these Special Energy cards in your deck before just putting in four of each one.

ENERGY

Scramble Energy Special Energy C

Scramble Energy can be attached only to an Evolved Pokémon (excluding Pokémon-ex). Scramble Energy provides ⊙ Energy. While in play, if you have more Prize cards left than your opponent, Scramble Energy provides every type of Energy but provides only 3 in any combination at a time. If the Pokémon Scramble Energy is attached to isn't an Evolved Pokémon (or evolves into Pokémon-ex), discard Scramble Energy.

511-C56-Z08   ©2006 Pokémon,

ENERGY

Double Rainbow Energy Special Energy Card

Double Rainbow Energy can be attached only to an Evolved Pokémon (excluding Pokémon-ex). While in play, Double Rainbow Energy provides every type of Energy but provides 2 Energy at a time. (Has no effect other than providing Energy.) Damage done to your opponent's Pokémon by the Pokémon Double Rainbow Energy is attached to is reduced by 10 (before applying Weakness and Resistance). When the Pokémon Double Rainbow Energy is attached to is no longer an Evolved Pokémon, discard Double Rainbow Energy.

Illus. Takumi Akabane

Y55-QC5-MUG   ©2006 Pokémon/Nintendo   88/100 ★

ENERGY

Call Energy   Special Energy Card

Call Energy provides ✶ Energy. Once during your turn, if the Pokémon Call Energy is attached to is your Active Pokémon, you may search your deck for up to 2 Basic Pokémon and put them onto your Bench. If you do, shuffle your deck and your turn ends.

Illus. Takumi Akabane

©2008 Pokémon/Nintendo   92/100 ◆

NAME: Gallade
SET: *Diamond & Pearl–Secret Wonders* (2007)

IT'S COOL BECAUSE: It has 130 HP, it has a good first attack that will send your opponent's Pokémon away for a bit after you hit it, and it has a second attack that could, if you use it early enough in the game, cause 180 damage all at once! This trick only works once, of course, but you can judge for yourself how many or how few Prize cards to flip over. If you had enough Prize cards left, you could do 100 damage three turns in a row!

Team Galactic's Wager from *Mysterious Treasures* could easily have been on this list because of how it messes up the game by making both you and your opponent start over with new hands. Sometimes it takes luck to win "Rock-Paper-Scissors," but sometimes you somehow know that your opponent is always going to choose "Rock"! This card was voted the number one card of 2007 by online players, so it's definitely worth your time to master your hand, literally!

#13

NAME: Infernape LV.*X*
SET: *Diamond & Pearl* (2007)

IT'S COOL BECAUSE: It does a lot of damage with its Flare Up attack (150 damage), which will Knock Out almost any Pokémon that Infernape LV.*X* might come up against. Even better, its Poké-Power gives you a chance to move Fire Energy cards from your deck into your discard pile to use with Flare Up. This gets easier each time because you're putting those eight Energy cards back into your deck . . . so you can find them again! Trainer cards like Felicity's Drawing will help you Flare Up even faster. So will Pokémon that let you discard Fire Energy cards attached to them to your discard pile, like Heatran from *Legends Awakened*.

WHAT'S IN A NAME? EKANS AND ARBOK

Some Pokémon names are easier to figure out than others. Koffing and Weezing? Pretty easy. Ekans and Arbok? A little harder, but just looking at them, you get the idea. Flip their names backwards (and pretend like the "k" in Arbok is a "c"), and suddenly their names make sense!

NAME: Absol
SET: *Diamond & Pearl–Secret Wonders* (2007)

IT'S COOL BECAUSE: As a basic Pokémon, Absol can come right into play and immediately start causing problems for your opponent. Many players play with lots of Trainer cards, so on the first turn you could easily be getting rid of at least one card (or maybe two cards) from your opponent's hand. That can be really effective so early in the game! Plus, its second attack has some chance to Knock Out your opponent's beginning Pokémon on the very first turn!

UNIQUE PEEK BACK: ANCIENT MEW

Ancient Mew! While the card couldn't be played—most people couldn't tell what it said, and the back of the card made it totally impossible to use—it was a popular holographic promo card when it came out in 2000 at the *Pokémon Movie* premiere. It's still pretty easy to get, and one of the most unusual cards in the entire Pokémon TCG.

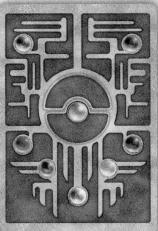

ANCIENT MEANING!

So, what does it all say on Ancient Mew? It has 30 HP, an attack called Psyche that does 40 damage for two Psychic Energy, Weakness to Psychic, no Resistance, and a Retreat Cost of two. Of course, that crazy back of the card is still going to make it hard for you to play with it, but you could always use card sleeves to disguise it!

#11

NAME: Pikachu
SET: E3 red cheeks (1999)

IT'S COOL BECAUSE: In May of 1999, promo cards of Pikachu were given away at the Electronic Entertainment Expo (E3) in Los Angeles. But a small number of those promo cards had a mistake on them—Pikachu had red cheeks instead of yellow ones. The red-cheek version quickly became a collector's item and continues to be one of the most valuable cards around. It's not a card you'd play with . . . but it's certainly one you'd want in your collection!

POP QUIZ!

Three Pokémon have names that read the same forward as they do backward. Can you name all three? Of course, you have nearly 500 names to think about, so here's a little help . . .

#1: Evolution Pokémon

#2: Rainbow Pokémon

#3: Long Neck Pokémon

Answer: Eevee, Ho-Oh, and Girafarig

NAME: Omastar
#10 **SET:** *Diamond & Pearl–Majestic Dawn* (2008)

IT'S COOL BECAUSE: Being able to devolve all of your opponent's Benched Evolved Pokémon is an extremely powerful ability, and Omastar gets to do it entirely for free. In combination with Pokémon that spread damage around on your opponent's Bench, Omastar's Primal Swirl Poké-Power becomes dangerous to even your opponent's best Pokémon. This is probably why it's popular!

CRUEL COMBO!

Once Omastar has put lots of your opponent's Evolution cards back in his or her hand (and maybe even *all* of those Evolution cards, if you play two Omastar on the same turn!), then it's time to pull out a mean trick: play Team Galactic's Wager (from *Mysterious Treasures*) to send your opponent's handful of Evolution cards back to his or her deck!

HONORABLE MENTION: OUT OF THE DARKNESS

Darkrai is quite a popular Pokémon, and its LV.X version (from *Great Encounters*) has some pretty good attacks (especially its Endless Darkness attack that can really cause your opponent a lot of sleepless nights when the Defending Pokémon won't wake up). Plus the card itself is valuable to collectors.

#9

NAME: Dark Persian
SET: Promo (2000)

IT'S COOL BECAUSE: Like the red-cheeks Pikachu from E3, Dark Persian comes with a little bit of a problem: the card had a mistake that led to it being recalled and printed correctly. And mistake cards, like other super-rare cards, are the favorites of collectors, so Dark Persian ranks pretty high on the list of all-time valuable cards. Of course, you have to have the version with the mistake on it . . .

MISS THE MISTAKE?

And you shouldn't have to look too hard to see the mistake on this promo card from a summer 2000 issue of *Nintendo Power Magazine*. Can you see the problem?

Answer: Dark Persian was supposed to have 60 HP . . . even if it made it out there without those Hit Points!

WHAT'S IN A NAME?
HITMON . . .

Hitmonchan and Hitmonlee.
Excellent fighters . . .

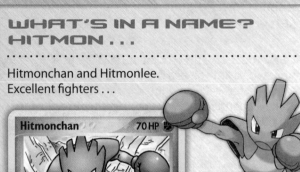

Hitmonchan 70 HP

BASIC

Poké-BODY **Stages of Evolution**
As long as Hitmonchan is an Evolved Pokémon, Hitmonchan gets +30 HP.

Heavy Punch
Does 10 damage times the number of your op Benched Pokémon.

Speedy Uppercut
This attack's damage isn't affected by W Resistance, Poké-Powers, Poké-Bodies, or any oth on the Defending Pokémon.

weakness   resistance   retreat

©2005 Pokémon/Nintendo

Hitmonlee 60 HP

BASIC

Poké-BODY **Stages of Evolution**
As long as Hitmonlee is an Evolved Pokémon, Hitmonlee's att 20 more damage to your opponent's Pokémon Weakness and Resistance).

tch Kick
of your opponent's Benched Pokémon. This does 10 damage to that Pokémon. (Don't apply Weakness and Resistance for Benched Pokémon.)

Mega Kick 40

weakness   resistance   retreat cost

©2005 Pokémon/Nintendo

. . . just like Jackie Chan and Bruce Lee, the fighters they're named for!

#8

NAME: Garchomp LV.*X*
SET: *Diamond & Pearl–Majestic Dawn* (2008)

IT'S COOL BECAUSE: Its Dragon Pulse Poké-Power is pretty good—you could do as much as 30 damage to each of your opponent's Benched Pokémon, but only the first time you play Garchomp LV.*X*. It's Garchomp's attack that makes this card so popular and valuable. Restore lets you take any Pokémon in your discard pile that's not a Pokémon LV.*X*, put in on your Bench as if it were a Basic Pokémon, and then attach up to three Energy cards from your discard pile to it—all for free. *Free*. And because Garchomp LV.*X* has no Retreat Cost, you can take that Pokémon your opponent worked so hard to Knock Out last turn and put it right back up there in the fight. For *free*. (Did I mention that you do all this for free?)

NAME: Celio's Network
SET: *EX Crystal Guardians* (2006)

IT'S COOL BECAUSE: Just about everybody who plays a winning deck has used this card at one time or another. It's perfect for finding almost any Pokémon you might need (except for Pokémon-ex), and really, there's almost always at least one Pokémon you could use to turn your game to victory. A very inexpensive card with a very useful effect.

DEJA VU COMBO!

Use Celio's Network to search for Persian (from *EX Delta Species*), because when Persian comes into play, you can use its Prowl Poké-Power to search for yet another card . . . like, say, another Celio's Network!

RAREST OF THE RARE: WORLD CHAMPIONSHIP CARD

Every August, a new Pokémon TCG World Champion is crowned (three Champions, actually, one in each of three age divisions). Those players who are on the top of their game receive a special one-of-a-kind (well, three-of-a-kind, actually!) Pokémon card: a World Champion card that no one else has! Though they aren't meant to be played in any deck, these cards are the rarest of the rare because they are the Champion's ticket to the next year's World Championships!

POKÉ-WEB SITES!

There are lots of places to get expert advice and insider scoop about everything related to the Pokémon Trading Card Game. Fans have created sites where the best players in the world talk about great cards, amazing decks, fun trivia, and just about anything you can think of about the Pokémon TCG. And the official Web site will give you the inside track on Pokémon Organized Play, the latest releases, demos so you can learn to play, and lots more! (Be sure to get your parent's permission before visiting the Web site.)

#6

NAME: Lugia ex
SET: *EX Unseen Forces* (2005)

IT'S COOL BECAUSE: Even the possibility of doing 200 damage made some players desperate to figure out how to use this card in a deck, and doing it for only 3 Energy makes it hard to resist! That's enough damage to take out even Wailord, which has the most HP of any Pokémon in the game—200. Lugia ex's Poké-Power isn't all that great, but it's Elemental Blast attack makes this a valuable collector's card!

NAME: Charizard ex
SET: *FireRed & LeafGreen* (2005)

IT'S COOL BECAUSE:
Another attack with big damage, and this time it's on an all-time favorite Pokémon, Charizard. This card is one collectors always seem to be searching for (and so it can be pretty expensive). It has a cool Poké-Body that makes sure all Energy attached to it is Fire Energy, since its Burn Down attack is going to cost you five Fire Energy. But for an unstoppable 200 damage? Most players who enjoy big, dramatic attacks love it when Charizard ex starts burning down the house!

HOT COMBO!

Try adding Boost Energy (from *EX Dragon Frontiers*) to Charizard ex. The three Colorless Energy that Boost Energy gives suddenly become Fire Energy. Since you have to discard Boost Energy at the end of the turn anyway, you get to do a sudden surprise attack that doesn't cost you as much!

POKÉ-HISTORY: BABY POKÉMON, E-CARDS, AND 1ST EDITION

A quick quiz (and some great trivia, in case you don't know the answers) about some card types that have come and gone in the Pokémon Trading Card Game:

1) What is name of the Baby Pokémon that evolves into Pikachu?

2) E-cards were regular cards that could be scanned into an E-Reader for additional Pokémon information. They began with the *Expedition* release (2002). What was the last set to contain these cards?

3) How many sets featured the unique "1ˢᵗ Edition" stamp that made cards more collectible? (Hint: the 1999 Base Set was the first set to feature this stamp, and 2002's *Neo Destiny* was the last!)

Sharpedo   70 HP

STAGE 1   Evolves from Carvanha

Poké-BODY Rough Skin
If Sharpedo is your Active Pokémon and is damaged by an opponent's attack (*even if Sharpedo is Knocked Out*), put 2 damage counters on the Attacking Pokémon.

Dark Slash   40+
You may discard a ⚫ Energy card attached to Sharpedo. If you do, this attack does 40 damage plus 30 more damage.

weakness   resistance   retreat cost

STAGE 2   Evolves from Machoke   Put Machamp

Machamp   10

Superpower Pokémon. Length: 5' 3", Weight: 287 lbs.

Pokémon Power: Strikes Back Whenever your opponent's attack damages Machamp (*even if Machamp is Knocked Out*), this power does 10 damage to the attacking Pokémon. (Don't apply Weakness and Resistance.) This power can't be used if Machamp is already Asleep, Confused, or Paralyzed when your opponent attacks.

Seismic Toss   60

weakness   resistance   retreat cost

Using its amazing muscles, it throws powerful punches that can knock its victim clear over the horizon. LV. 67 #68

Answers: 1) Pichu; Baby Pokémon were introduced in Neo Genesis (2000) with some special rules of their own, but they've now become Basic Pokémon. **2)** EX Dragon (2003) was the last set to feature the e-cards, so they appeared in six sets altogether. **3)** Ten sets in all featured the 1st Edition stamp, meaning you'd try to collect 20 sets if you wanted a 1st Edition and an Unlimited card from each set!

NAME: Glaceon LV.*X*
SET: *Diamond & Pearl–Majestic Dawn* (2008)

IT'S COOL BECAUSE: Lots of popular, winning decks count on the Poké-Powers of their Pokémon to make other things happen—to search for cards, to move Energy around, and lots of other clever twists and combos. But if you have Glaceon LV.*X* as your Active Pokémon, a lot of your opponent's tricks will come to a halt! This only works, of course, as long as you're ready to fight with Glaceon LV.*X*. Fortunately, it's a good fighter. Its Avalanche attack does at least 70 to your opponent's Defending Pokémon, and it could do as much total damage as 90 to 170 damage, if you win your coin flip. And with a low Retreat Cost, you can take Glaceon LV.*X* out of the battle if things get too rough!

NAME: Gardevoir LV.*X*
SET: *Diamond & Pearl–Secret Wonders* (2008)

IT'S COOL BECAUSE: One thing never to forget about LV.*X* Pokémon is that they can use all the attacks and Poké-Bodies and Poké-Powers of the cards underneath them—in this case, Gardevoir and Kirlia. So, if Gardevoir LV.*X* is played on Gardevoir from *Secret Wonders*, you get even more good stuff going on! Gardevoir LV.*X*'s Bring Down attack lets you take out another Pokémon in play (try hard not to make it your own!). The Gardevoir underneath it gives you the Poké-Power Telepass to use a Supporter card from your opponent's discard pile or Gardevoir's Psychic Lock attack to shut down your opponent's Poké-Powers. And then there's the Kirlia underneath *that* to consider . . . why, there are all kinds of possibilities! A popular, exciting, and fun card to play with!

TINS AND 2-PACKS AND PROMOS, OH MY!

There are lots of places to find Pokémon cards that are a little harder to collect than others. Promo cards are often added to Pokémon products like holiday tins (which are also cool for keeping your cards in) and two-pack or three-pack products. You can also collect cool promo cards at events like Prereleases and leagues, and in 2008, you could collect 12 cards through Burger King® Kids Meals!

Grotle Lv.21 HP 90

STAGE 1 Evolves from Turtwig

DIAMOND & PEARL

Synthesis
Search your deck for a Energy card and attach it to 1 of your Pokémon. Shuffle your deck afterward.

Cut 50

It lives along water in forests. In the daytime, it leaves the forest to sunbathe its tree shell.

Happiny Lv.8 HP 60

BASIC

DIAMOND & PEARL

Poké-POWER Baby Evolution
Once during your turn (before your attack), you may put Chansey from your hand onto Happiny (this counts as evolving Happiny) and remove all damage counters from Happiny.

Lively
Remove 2 damage counters from 1 of your Pokémon.

It loves round white things. It carries an egg-shaped rock in imitation of its MAMA.

Lucario Lv.30 HP 90

STAGE 1 Evolves from Riolu

DIAMOND & PEARL

Feint 30
This attack's damage isn't affected by Resistance.

Aura Sphere 40
Does 20 damage to 1 of your opponent's Benched Pokémon. (Don't apply Weakness and Resistance for Benched Pokémon.)

It has the ability to sense the auras of all things. It understands human speech.

Manaphy Lv.20 HP 70

BASIC

DIAMOND & PEARL

Call for Family
Search your deck for a Basic Pokémon and put it onto your Bench. Shuffle your deck afterward.

Aqua Ring 30
Switch Manaphy with 1 of your Benched Pokémon.

Born on a cold seafloor, it will swim great distances to return to its birthplace.

Pikachu Lv.15 HP 60

BASIC

DIAMOND & PEARL

Poké-POWER Electro Recycle
Once during your turn (before your attack), if Pichu is anywhere under Pikachu, you may search your discard pile for a Energy card, show it to your opponent, and put it into your hand. This power can't be used if Pikachu is affected by a Special Condition.

BikaBika 20+
Flip a coin. If heads, this attack does 20 damage plus 10 more damage.

It lives in forests with others. It stores electricity in the pouches in its cheeks.

NAME: Time-Space Distortion

SET: *Diamond & Pearl–Mysterious Treasures* (2007)

IT'S COOL BECAUSE: First, it's rarer than rare (and it has a wacky number—#124/123), which already makes it popular with collectors. It has cool art. But more than anything, it's just plain powerful. You can have four of them in your deck, and if one of your best Stage 2 Pokémon was Knocked Out and is in the discard pile, you might be able to get its whole Evolution chain back into your hand with just three coin flips!

Some players think Night Maintenance (which puts cards from your discard pile back into your deck) is better because it guarantees you'll see the Pokémon you chose again. Sure, it will . . . if you can last long enough to draw them! But Time-Space Distortion has an 87.5% chance of putting at least one Pokémon right back into your hand!

COMBINATION LOCK!

Infernape LV.X (*Diamond & Pearl*) has a great attack—Flare Up, which does 150 damage for only two Fire Energy. But it requires you to get eight Fire Energy cards out of your discard pile to make it work; otherwise, it doesn't do anything! But never fear: Delcatty (*EX Power Keepers*) lets you discard an Energy card from your hand every single turn while drawing three more cards from your deck.

Delcatty   **70 HP** ⭐

Illus. Masakazu Fukuda

STAGE 1   Evolves from Skitty

Poké-POWER   **Energy Draw**

Once during your turn (*before your attack*), you may discard 1 Energy card from your hand. Then draw up to 3 cards from your deck. This power can't be used if Delcatty is affected by a Special Condition.

Energy Source   10x

...mage times the amount of Energy ...all of your Active Pokémon.

resistance   retreat cost

8/108 ★ ©

©2007 Pokémon/Nintendo

Infernape LV.X   HP 120 🔥

LEVEL-UP Put onto Infernape

Poké-POWER   **Burning Head**

Once during your turn (*before your attack*), you may look at the top 3 cards of your deck, choose 1 of them, and put it into your hand. Discard the other 2 cards. This power can't be used if Infernape is affected by a Special Condition.

🔥🔥   **Flare Up**   150

Search your discard pile for 8 🔥 Energy cards, show them to your opponent, and shuffle them into your deck. (This attack does nothing if you don't have 8 🔥 Energy cards in your discard pile.)

Put this card onto your active Infernape. Infernape LV.X can use any attack, Poké-Power, or Poké-Body from its previous Level.

Illus. 5hin-ow

weakness   🌊+30   resistance   retreat cost

©2007 Pokémon/Nintendo   121/130

#1

NAME: Charizard
SET: Base Set (1998; 1st Edition)

IT'S COOL BECAUSE: When the game first began, Charizard was the most sought-after card of all because of its amazing Fire Spin attack, which did an impressive 100 damage. That would be enough to Knock Out almost every other Pokémon with just one attack!

Plus, the Base Set came with a limited 1st-Edition stamp on it, and there weren't very many cards printed with that special stamp on it. Its value goes up and down, but it's still one of the most expensive cards to collect. So, over the years, this Charizard has become a legend because of how hard it is to catch!

A HORSE OF A DIFFERENT COLOR: BELLA SARA

Collect. Activate. Play. That's the idea behind the Bella Sara trading cards, which provide players and collectors a whole new way to enjoy their cards: online! Each of the beautiful horse-themed cards in Bella Sara comes with a code that unlocks a virtual version of that same horse at **www.BellaSara.com**. At the Web site, you can earn horseshoes to trade for all sorts of other fun objects, and find horse jumping and riding games, puzzles, coloring books, interactive storybooks, cottages that you can decorate yourself, and lots more.

Inspired by her daughter's love for horses, creator Gitte Odder Brændgaard brought Bella Sara to life as a way to encourage kids to accept and express their feelings. "Beauty comes from within" is the game's main message—and Bella Sara offers positive thoughts through uplifting notes on every card.

Over 50 million cards have been sold worldwide and nearly three million registered users from more than 240 countries have joined the free Bella Sara online world. One pack is all it takes to enter Bella Sara's magical world—a world where you can make amazing new friends. Collect your favorite horses and get ready to be the hero in your own story!

NAME: Beran
SET: *Magical Friends* (2008)

YOU SHOULD KNOW: Beran (whose name is short for *beranu*, which is the Sardinian word for "spring") is inspired by the Green Man, a figure from European folklore who represents spring. When spring comes to North of North, that's when Beran of the Great Forest joins with his friends, the Twinkle Imps, to bring about all the changes of the season.

BERAN'S FAMILY

In the *Baby Bella* set, Beran and Rosebriar are featured with their three foals: Briar, Calyx, and Petal.

NAME: Colour
SET: 2nd Series (2007)

YOU SHOULD KNOW: Colour's message to "Feel the joy in what you see, hear, and sense" is to remind you of the importance of experiencing life through all your perceptions. When you are aware of the beauty in the world, your life becomes better for it! With a flowing rainbow mane, Colour is the most-activated card in the 2nd Series set!

2ND SERIES, FIRST LOOK!

The 2nd Series of Bella Sara cards includes new takes on the cards from the hard-to-find First Series set, plus new flying and swimming horses. Only five cards from the First Series didn't make it into the 2nd Series: Ghost, Shadow, Starfighter, Sunny, and Sweety.

Ghost
Your beauty comes from within
SZP4BE8K6L

Shadow
*Look within yourself
and love what you find there.*
SZP4BE8K6L

Starfighter
*Believe in your vision
and make it come true.*
SZP4BE8K6L

Sunny
*The wind blows. The sun is shining.
Surround yourself with positive friends.*
SZP4BE8K6L

Sweety
*You are a perfect child.
Believe it.*
SZP4BE8K6L

NAME: Athena
SET: *Ancient Lights* (2007)

#23

YOU SHOULD KNOW: Athena is named for the Greek goddess of wisdom and is one of the most important horses in the *Ancient Lights* set. She also appears in the *Baby Bella* set with her mate, Apollo. Together, they have two foals—Aegis and Harmony.

Athena
*Be yourself, be free, and allow
others the same freedom.*
FJ3L82NBV4
Play with this horse online! Enter this code at www.bellasara.com
Artwork by Spooze. © 2006–2007 conceptcard. All rights reserved.

THE FOUR WINDS

Four promotional cards were released to support *Ancient Lights*. They were named for the Greek gods of the four winds, who took the form of winged horses to draw the god Zeus's chariot. Boreas is the wintry North Wind, Euros is the East Wind of autumn, Notos is the South Wind of summer thunderstorms, and Zephyros is the gentle West Wind of spring.

 #22

NAME: Lillova
SET: *Magical Friends* (2008)

YOU SHOULD KNOW:
Lillova's name means "Little Gift" in Old Norse, which is the perfect name for this miniature horse with dragonfly wings. Her magical friend, the sweetpea reindeer, is almost the same size! With fantastic art, the shiny card Lillova is a fan favorite!

Lillova
Love has no conditions.

RD68-7428-SD90-M2F3

BFF

Magical Friends was the first set to focus on North of North, the world of Bella Sara. Some of the cards show landmarks in North of North. For example, the art for Mellonie shows the Bella and Bello Monuments in the background. Every horse in this set has a magical friend of his or her very own, more than 70 in all!

NAME: Jewel
SET: First Series (2006)

YOU SHOULD KNOW: In the world of Bella Sara, Jewel is a legendary horse, created after being sculpted from stone rich in gold and gems and brought to life by Sara's magic. She has had a book written about her—*Jewel's Magic*—and she has been featured in every Bella Sara set so far!

JEWEL'S MUSIC BOX

In the *Magical Friends* set, all of the Energy cards are toys because the set is all about baby horses, or foals. Jewel's Music Box (which has a sculpture of Jewel on its top) plays beautiful music and sparkles with jewels and light when you activate it at the Bella Sara Web site.

#20

NAME: Petal
SET: *Baby Bella* (2008)

YOU SHOULD KNOW: The daughter of Rosebriar and Beran—her coat echoes Beran's body patterns in green—Petal was born in the same rose garden where her mother and father met. When she was born, she was surrounded by Rose Dragons. (You can see a pair of Rose Dragons in the art.) She is named for the rose petals those Rose Dragons attached to her mane and tail when she walked for the first time.

BABY BELLA

The *Baby Bella* set introduced lots of new ideas to the Bella Sara game: 1) horse families, (which changed the layout of the cards to make room for family information), 2) toy cards instead of energy cards, 3) teacher horses that educate the foals in North of North, and 4) dual-horse cards for all the parent cards. In fact, the art for Embarr and Freja, Arim, and Mira was created to fit together as one family!

#19

NAME: Iceking
SET: *Northern Lights* (2007)

YOU SHOULD KNOW:
Iceking—the first horse in Bella Sara made from ice—lives on the Whitemantle Glacier in North of North. Though he appeared in *Northern Lights* the first time, he also appears with his mate, Nyx, and their three foals (Iceprince, Starfrost, and Toboggan) in the *Baby Bella* set.

Iceking
Hope is like magic. It keeps you full of energy.
SZP48E8K6L

LEGENDS!

The four promotional cards for *Northern Lights* were inspired by the four legendary treasures of Ireland. Erinn has the Lia Fáil (Stone of Destiny), Lugh has the Spear Lúin (Flaming Spear), Nuada has the Claíomh Solais (Sword of Light), and Brigid has the Coire Anseasc (Dagda's Cauldron). The Danu card also depicts all four treasures!

Erinn
Know yourself and you will know others.
SZP48E8K6L

Lugh
Use your quick mind to solve your problems.
SZP48E8K6L

Nuada
There is no magic stronger than trying again.
SZP48E8K6L

Brigid
Be the kind of person the world needs.
SZP48E8K6L

#18

NAME: Finling
SET: *Magical Friends*
(2008)

YOU SHOULD KNOW: The finling is a magical friend of the deep oceans. It has a light on the end of a stalk so it can see in the inky blackness. When you activate this card online, you get your own finling that sleeps, blows bubbles, and tries to catch a fish! You can also read about a finling in three chapters of one of the online storybooks, "Best of Friends."

Finling

RD68-7428-SD90-M2F3

Use this card online! Enter this code at www.bellasara.com
Artwork by Tanya Mendicht © 2005-2006 conceptcard. All rights reserved.

BELLA SARA ONLINE

The Bella Sara Web site not only has storybooks and stables, it also has easy-to-understand video explanations of all that you can do and discover in North of North, the world of Bella Sara. You'll find an explanation of horseshoes and how you get them, how to care for your horse, and how to decorate your cottage. You'll also learn about caring for your horses in your stables, whether they are Land, Air, or Sea stables! You can also find a store locator to help you find businesses near your home where you can buy Bella Sara cards.

#17

NAME: Bellisimo
SET: *Baby Bella* (2008)

YOU SHOULD KNOW:
Bellisimo is the foal of Bella and Bello. He was born by the shores of the same lake where his mother and father first met. (His coloring is a mix of their two coats, Bella's white and Bello's black.) "Trust yourself and you will know how to live" is Bellisimo's popular message.

Trust yourself and you will know how to live.
Parents: Bello & Bella
RD68-7428-SD90-M2F3
Play online! Enter this code at www.bellasara.com

SARA, THE GODDESS OF HORSES

Sara and her parents were magical beings who lived among the mortals in North of North when the Bella Sara story begins. It was her first encounter with a herd of horses led by the magnificent white mare Bella that put Sara on the path to loving and caring for horses always. The first time she touched Bella, they were both magically transformed into the model for bonds between children and horses for all future generations. You can read more about Bella and Sara in the upcoming book, *The Ultimate Guide to the World of Bella Sara.*

#16

NAME: Amor
SET: *Ancient Lights* (2007)

Amor
Use your love to bring peace to the world.

SZP48E8K6L
Play with this horse online! Enter this code at www.bellasara.com
Artwork by Jennifer Meyer. © 2005-2007 conceptcard. All rights reserved.

YOU SHOULD KNOW: Amor is an air horse who once spread peace throughout a war-torn land through an act of love and kindness that, by the care of a soldier, reunited a little girl with her mother. That singular act of selfless love spread from one person to another, from deed to deed, until the chain finally reached the king of the land, who stopped the fighting.

THE ART OF LOVE

The artwork for Amor—who's named for the god of love—shows two bunnies kissing. This image was made into online objects that appeared in players' cottages on Valentine's Day.

#15

NAME: Ghost
SET: First Series (2006)

Ghost
Your beauty comes from within.

SZP48E8K6L
Play with this horse online! Enter this code at www.bellasara.com
Artwork by Marie Nyman. © 2005-2006 conceptcard. All Rights Reserved.   8/55

YOU SHOULD KNOW: The ethereal horse Ghost bears the Bella Sara game's central message: "Your beauty comes from within." Ghost's most unique feature is that she is blind; she has no eyes. And this represents her message: beauty is a quality that is expressed rather than seen.

ARTS AND LETTERS

On **www.BellaSara.com**, you can find unique art drawn by other Bella Sara fans just like you. With your parent's permission, you can send in your own fan art! You can find the address to mail it on the official Bella Sara Web site.

Also on the Web site, you can find questions written to the *real* Sara . . . and her answers. You can write to her, too!

NAME: Cheyenne
#14

SET: *Native Lights* (2008)

YOU SHOULD KNOW:
Cheyenne gets his name from the Native American tribe of the same name. He is a mighty warrior of the plains who helps others in distress, and with his animal companion, Eagle, he has learned to see the world from a different point of view. Though he's a loner, he still loves others. He is shy when anyone shows affection for him.

Cheyenne
*See the beauty in both the
shadow and the light.*

SZP4BE8K6L

Play with this horse online! Enter this code at www.bellasara.com
Artwork by Sporps. © 2005-2008 conceptguard. All rights reserved.

NAME: Fiona
SET: First Series (2006)

YOU SHOULD KNOW: Fiona was created by Sara when, after telling a story, Sara tossed a page from the Patchwork into a roaring fire. Fiona was born from that fire and went on to become one of the four legendary horses in the world of Bella Sara. Her message to "Be the hero of your own story" is reflected in the storybook castle in her portrait.

Fiona
Be the hero in your own story.

S2P48E8K6L
Play with this horse online! Enter this code at www.bellasara.com
Artwork by Tarja Kettunen. © 2005-2006 unexpected. All Rights Reserved. F4/9

THE GROWING WORLD

From First Series through *Baby Bella*, there are 440 cards in the Bella Sara game so far. Three more sets come out every year, and in 2009, the world will grow with the release of *Treasures*, *Royalty*, and *Bella's Ball*!

NAME: Venus
SET: *Ancient Lights*
(2007)

YOU SHOULD KNOW: Venus is named for the goddess of love and beauty in Roman mythology. Though she is not a water horse, Venus can swim like one. Her image reflects the sea with seaweed, shells, and pearls. As the most activated non-common card in the entire *Ancient Lights* set, many players have found her message to "Spread your joy around for all the share" to be a virtue worth sharing, indeed!

Venus
Spread your joy around for all to share.

SAF48E8K6L
Play with this horse online! Enter this code at www.bellasara.com
Artwork by zpooge. © 2005-2007 unexpected. All rights reserved.

PART OF THE LIGHTS?

They all have names that would fit well with the other horses in *Ancient Lights*. But which of these horses does *not* appear in the set?

A) Artemis

C) Pegasus

B) Hercules

D) All of the above

#11

NAME: Bello
SET: First Series (2006)

YOU SHOULD KNOW: Bello, Bella's mate, was part of the First Herd that Sara ever saw and is one of the most popular horses in the Bella Sara game. He's also the father of Bellisimo and has appeared in four different sets so far!

Bello
Life is a gift.
Receive it and love it.

S2P48E8K6L

Play with this horse online! Enter this code at www.bellasara.com
Artwork by Tanja Kurizedüki ©2005-2006 concpound. All Rights Reserved. F3/9

STORIES TO TELL

Beginning in December 2008, you'll be able to read adventures about some of the horses in the world of Bella Sara. *Bella's Gift, Nike's Great Race, Jewel's Magic,* and *Valkrist's Flight* are the first four stories scheduled to be published, with more to come!

Answer: D) Artemis appears in the First Series and 2nd Series; Hercules appears in the First Series, 2nd Series, and Baby Bella; and Pegasus appears in 2nd Series and Baby Bella.

#10

NAME: Tomtomme
SET: *Magical Friends* (2008)

. . . .

YOU SHOULD KNOW:
Tomtommes are frisky, mouse-like creatures with musical sensibilities. Their tails beat back and forth to keep time. They can make music with their ears, which—in addition to eating cheese!—your own tomtomme will do when you activate one online! You can also read about the tomtomme Tyler in an online storybook!

Tomtomme

RD68-7428-SD90-M2F3
Use this card online! Enter this code at www.bellasara.com
Artwork by Peter Mosáefo © 2005–2008 conceptard. All rights reserved.

HORSES, FRIENDS . . . AND HUMANS?

As of the *Baby Bella* set, only one U.S. horse card has a human in the art: Fylgie in *Northern Lights* shows a sleeping girl dreaming of herself with Fylgie. You can also find humans on two energy cards: Riding Lesson in both the First Series and 2nd Series and Anvil & Hammer from *Northern Lights*!

#9

NAME: Steampoppo
SET: *Magical Friends* (2008)

YOU SHOULD KNOW: Steampoppos live in the deepest jungles of the tropical regions of North of North, where they live on a steady diet of banas. What's a bana? It's looks like a banana, but it tastes like walnut fudge! Your own Steampoppo will blow steam from its nose and eat banas when you activate it online.

Steampoppo

RD68-7428-5D90-M2F3

NAME THAT FRIEND!

Can you guess the two words that were combined to make the name "Steampoppo"?

#8

NAME: Lien
SET: *Magical Friends* (2008)

YOU SHOULD KNOW: "Lien" means "lotus" in Vietnamese, and you can see that lotuses grow on Lien. She is the first elemental water horse, with a body made entirely of water—if you watch her closely, you can see fish she has accidentally picked up swimming inside of her! Some believe that her friendship with lotus hedgehogs has kept her from dissolving into a dream.

Lien
The most important time in your life is right now.
RD68-7428-5D90-M2F3

Answer: "Steam" and "hippopotamus"!

57

 # 7

NAME: Janie
SET: *Baby Bella* (2008)

YOU SHOULD KNOW: If you know your Bella Sara horses well, you might recognize that Janie has the look and coloring of her mother, Ondine, but her father Flipper's shape. She was born into a beautiful bubble under the sea, and it's under the sea where she loves to explore the hidden caves where her parents sometimes go. Janie is named after the daughter of the artist who created the card.

SECRET MESSAGES REVEALED

Look closely at some cards, and you might find words hidden in the art. In the 2nd Series, you can find the Chinese characters for "One who knows no fear" in the art for Yung, the name "Bella" in Japanese in Konfu's picture, and the Chinese character for "horse" in the art of Mushu. And in *Northern Lights*, you can find runes on the Brisi card that mean "Let love guide you."

#6

NAME: Nike
SET: *Ancient Lights*
(2007)

YOU SHOULD KNOW: Like Thunder, Jewel, and Fiona, Nike is one of the four legendary horses in the world of Bella Sara. She's named for the winged goddess of victory from Greek mythology. She was born on Mount Olympus among the horse herds of the Greek gods. You can see her magic reflected in the angelic butterfly fairies that circle her and the multicolored gossamer ribbons she wears.

Nike
Have the courage to trust yourself.

SZP48E8K6L

ALWAYS MORE TO SEE . . .

In the *Baby Bella* set, the "fish" in the Crystal Fishbowl card art is really a fire spoops, one of Edana's magical friends. The Lullaby Panda is a toy version of the tea-leaf panda that is Cha Ye's magical friend, and the Waterpearl Tadpole is a toy version of the neon tadpole that is Waterpearl's magical friend!

A RARE BREED

Some cards in the Bella Sara game are harder to collect than others; these are called rare cards. Some cards are even rarer than those; they're called shiny cards. Out of the 64 cards in the First Series, only nine are shiny cards. There are 27 shiny cards in the 2nd Series. Shiny cards are randomly mixed in with all the regular cards you find in booster packs and other releases of the Bella Sara game!

#5

NAME: Anemone
SET: *Magical Friends* (2008)

YOU SHOULD KNOW: Anemone lives high in the sky, as is fitting for one whose name comes from the Greek word meaning "windflower," Anemoi. Whiffle bears have befriended her, as you can see in the art (which was voted a fan favorite). Together, the whiffle bears and Anemone "herd clouds" to send rainclouds over farms during dry spells or to send them away from places where people are enjoying picnics.

Anemone
*Keep your heart open.
Believe in getting and giving love.*
RD68-7428-5D90-H2F3

MAGICAL MENTIONS!

Magical Friends was the first set to include a checklist in the card packs to help you keep track of all the cards you want to collect. It was also the first set not to have energy cards; it has friend cards instead!

#4

NAME: Osage
SET: *Native Lights*
(2008)

YOU SHOULD KNOW:
Named after the Osage
Native American tribe that
lived on the Great Plains,
Osage received the gift of
an independent spirit from
her animal companion,
butterfly. "Be free to change
your mind" is the message
of this most activated non-
common card in the entire
Native Lights set.

Osage
Be free to change your mind.

SZP48E8K6L

HORSESHOES!

Horseshoes are your key to adding more to your stables
and cottage when you get permission to go to the Bella
Sara Web site. You can buy horseshoes from the Horseshoe
Shop, you can earn them by playing games like Magic
Bubble Wand and the Firelight Festival, and you can earn
them by activating Bella Sara trading cards. Each time you
activate a card you earn more horseshoes: Common cards
equal 25 horseshoes, rare cards equal 100 horseshoes,
energy cards equal 150 horseshoes, and shiny cards equal
250 horseshoes!

POKÉMON

BELLA SARA

NARUTO

YU-GI-OH!

BAKUGAN

3

NAME: Ondine
SET: *Magical Friends (2008)*

YOU SHOULD KNOW: "Make every day an adventure!" From the hidden pools and glades where she lives, Ondine—who was named after mythological water nymphs—lives by her own message. She is able to run across water as if it were land, and with her bubble turtle friends, she's able to fly using their magical bubbles! You can also find her, along with her mate, Flipper, and their foal Janie, in the *Baby Bella* set. Ondine and Flipper also have another foal, Murttie.

Ondine
Make every day an adventure!

RD68-7428-5D90-M2F3

SKIRNISMOL

What does that mean? Well, it's the name of an ancient Icelandic poem. The runes that appear in the art for Firewalker from *Northern Lights* are taken from this poem.

The horse will I give thee

That goes through the dark

And magic flickering flames,

And the sword as well

That will fight of itself

If a worthy hero wields it.

Firewalker
Belief gives you the courage to move forward and take chances.

SZP48E8K6L

NAME: Bella & Bello
SET: *Baby Bella* (2008)

. . . .

YOU SHOULD KNOW: This is the first time Bella and Bello appear together on a card. When they met, their noses touched and a great wind blew out of the north, setting destiny in motion. They knew they would be together forever. Their shared message is "Life is a gift. Feel the bliss of joy and energy that comes with it."

TWO FOR ONE!

. . . .

In the 2nd Series, you can find two cards that are called dual-horse cards; you get both horses when you activate them! There's Friends, which gives you the horses Amy and Amity, and you can also find the dual-horse card Yin and Yang.

MAGICAL CODE!

· ·

The wonder of Bella Sara is not just the cards you can collect, but also the online world you can explore. Every card in the Bella Sara game comes with a unique code for you to entire online at **www.BellaSara.com**. But here's a special code just for you right now:

BEL#-2342-5678

This will unlock some special surprises for you that you can't find anywhere else! Be sure to get your parent's permission before visiting the Bella Sara Web site.

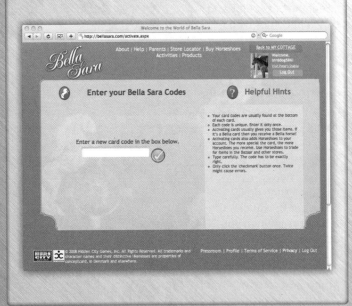

NAME: Bella
SET: *Magical Friends* (2008)

YOU SHOULD KNOW: Bella appears in every set of Bella Sara cards. Named for the creator's daughter Sara's horse, she is the most popular of all the Bella Sara horses. In the card from *Magical Friends*, Bella is shown with a rare Starstone Otter, which is named for the pendant she wears. The Starstone Otter shows herself only to those who have a great purpose, and she and Bella have been friends for many years. So . . . what do you think Bella's great purpose is?

Bella
Think positive every day! Feel the bliss of joy and energy that comes with it.

RD68–7428–SD90–M2F3

Play with this horse online! Enter this code at www.bellasara.com

Artwork by Cindy Price. © 2005–2008 conceptcard. All rights reserved.

NINJAS RULE IN THE NARUTO COLLECTIBLE CARD GAME!

At the core of the Ninja-based collectible card game Naruto is the title character, Naruto Uzumaki, who is on a quest to become Hokage, the protector of his village. Naruto is accompanied by many friends and allies—some of whom are not always what they seem—but he keeps a secret from all of them that might change his future: a dangerous spirit, the Nine-Tailed Fox, lives inside of him. And this spirit could sway him from his chosen path.

Based on the successful manga books by Masashi Kishimoto, the Naruto CCG lets you play with Naruto, his friend and rival Sasuke, their friend Sakura, and even villains like the sinister Orochimau. Combining your Ninjas with the various Ninja arts on Jutsu cards, you'll undertake Missions, launch attacks, battle teams of your opponent's Ninjas, defend your village, and earn Battle Rewards. Ten Battle Rewards and you are the victor!

Since 2006, ten different sets of Naruto cards have been released, giving thousands of would-be Ninjas a chance to build decks out of the hundreds of cards available. And the organized play community is amazing—players go from being novices, or genin, all the way to playing in the annual Sannin tournament in August, where they can prove their skills to the entire world!

To get started, pick up a starter set—which comes with a 40-card deck, 10 extra cards (called sideboard cards), a coin, turn markers, and an instruction manual. Everything you need to start battling Ninja-style!

NAME: Jonin's Intervention
FIRST APPEARED: *Series 3: Curse of the Sand* (2006)

WHY PLAY WITH IT: Sure, putting out tiny Genin Ninjas on turns 0, 1, and 2 is nice, but how about putting a huge Jonin like Kakashi or Might Guy out on the first turn? Strong enough to have its own deck-type, Jonins' Intervention (often referred to as "JI") was, at one time, one of the strongest decks played. Now JI is played as a subtype, allowing Fire decks to claim control of the game early. Plus, who doesn't want the biggest Ninja being able to play the best Jutsu out before everything else?

"Why are you and the other Jonin butting in?!"

Jonins' Intervention 1 1

Effect: When any of your Ninjas are discarded after being in play during this turn, you can move 1 "Jonin" Ninja from your hand to your Village.

作 106   © 2002 MASASHI KISHIMOTO

COMBOS!

This card works great with Nawaki, a little Genin that discards on his own at the end of the turn, letting you draw an extra card!

"Tsunade, could this be ..."

Nawaki ⓪ ⓪

Leaf | Genin | Male

[12TH BIRTHDAY]
When this Ninja is put in play, draw 1 card.
Valid: Discard this Ninja and draw 1 card at the end of the turn it is put in play.

0/0

2/0

209 © 2002 MASASHI KISHIMOTO

#24

NAME: Changes in Pairings
FIRST APPEARED: *Series 4:
Revenge and Rebirth* (2007)

WHY PLAY WITH IT:
Originally thought by players to be just an "okay" card, this card quickly gave rise to a new deck-type called "Tempo." Using cards like Changes in Pairings, Pass Permit, and Clients such as Emi, "Tempo" was made to get around an opponent's Ninjas to attack your opponent for direct damage, quickly ending the game in a matter of three to four turns. Now that's speed!

NAME: The Third Hokage
FIRST APPEARED: *Series 4: Revenge and Rebirth* (2007)

WHY PLAY WITH IT:
The Third Hokage, once the most powerful Ninja in the Leaf Village, also has one of the most powerful abilities in the game. Being able to remove another Ninja from play entirely at the drop of a hat allows The Third Hokage to negate powerful Jutsu cards being used by the Ninja, and could also allow your Ninjas to attack your opponent directly!

THE MEANING OF "HOKAGE"

What does it mean to be Hokage? The title is only given to the most powerful Ninja in the Leaf Village. From the small beginnings of the village, only five Hokages have been named so far. Each Hokage brings special strengths that have allowed the Leaf Village to grow stronger with each generation.

#22

NAME: Haku
FIRST APPEARED: *Series 6: Eternal Rivalry* (2007)

WHY PLAY WITH IT: Haku, the right-hand man of Zabuza Momochi, Demon of the Cloud Village, protects your other Ninjas from your opponent's Jutsu cards by injuring them temporarily. Many players in certain areas swear by this card as being one of the best ways to protect your Ninjas and to give yourself a distinct advantage in power.

"If I hadn't intervened, you'd be dead now ... that much is certain."

Haku

Mist | Rougue Ninja | Male

[CAMOUFLAGE]
You can change 1 other Ninja in this Ninja's Team to injured status. In that case, that Ninja cannot be targeted by your opponent's Jutsu cards during the turn. Heal that injured Ninja at the end of the turn.

© 2002 MASASHI KISHIMOTO

4/3

ONE CARD TOO FEW? DRAW MORE!

Haku is played primarily with a client named Futaba. By using Haku's effect, you can draw an extra card at the end of every turn. For those players who feel that one card a turn just isn't enough, Haku + Futaba drawing comes in handy!

"Someone precious?"

Futaba

Leaf | Ninja Academy Student | Female

Effect: Everytime you heal 1 of your injured Ninjas, draw 1 card.

依 019 © 2002 MASASHI KISHIMOTO

DID YOU KNOW?

Masashi Kishimoto, the creator of the Naruto manga and universe, frequently cites other anime artists as influences, including the creator of Dragonball® and Dragonball Z®, Akira Toriyama. Interested in Dragonball? Check out the Bandai Web site and click on "Dragonball" to check out the newest Dragonball CCG with your parent's permission!

#21

NAME: Chidori
FIRST APPEARED: *Series 4:*
Revenge and Rebirth (2007)

WHY PLAY WITH IT: Aside from being Sasuke's signature move, Chidori is brutally powerful, enough to allow a single Ninja to wipe out a team of three. Many players combined this card with the Third Hokage (#23 on this list) to maintain complete battle control in the game.

CHIDORI?

Lightning Blade has already been translated into English, but do you know what "Chidori" means?

Answer: Chidori = 1,000 birds. The name was given to signify the sound that the Jutsu makes when it's used.

#20

NAME: Sakura's Decision
FIRST APPEARED: *Series 3: Curse of the Sand* (2006)

WHY PLAY WITH IT: This card gets better and better with every set that's released. All that is required is a Ninja with the Female characteristic, and you get to draw cards! Although it's named Sakura's Decision, many people have taken a liking to using the card with the Shikamaru Nara & Temari Platoon card.

"Now it's my turn to take the lead. And all of you can watch me from the background."

Sakura's Decision 2 1

Target: 1 of your healthy "Female" Ninjas

Effect: Injure the target. Then, draw the same number of cards as the target's "Mental Power".

作 080 © 2002 MASASHI KISHIMOTO

作戦 MISSION

風 WIND

"Now...
watch

Sa

Targe

Effec
cards

作 080

忍 NINJA

風 WIND

土 EARTH

"Now, what do you think?" "....."

♦ Shikamaru Nara & Temari 3 0

Leaf | Sand | Genin | Chunin | Male | Female | Platoon
Mental Power: 5

[STRONG-ARM TACTICS]
During the Exchange of Jutsu, you can discard 2 of your Chakras. In that case, choose one of the following: This Ninja's Team and the Team Battling against this Ninja's Team perform a Mental Power Battle during the turn OR This Ninja's Team and your opponent's Team Battling against this Ninja's Team cannot perform a Mental Power Battle during the turn.

0/3

4/4

忍 264   © 2002 MASASHI KISHIMOTO • • •

SHADOW/ WEAPON

NAME: Shikamaru Nara & Temari
FIRST APPEARED: *Series 8: Battle of Destiny* (2008)

WHY PLAY WITH IT:
On the turn it can be put into play, this platoon has absolutely phenomenal stats. More important, this platoon also works especially well with Sakura's Decision (#20 in our countdown), allowing you to draw five cards with a single Mission card. Add to this the fact that this Ninja can make Mental Power battles, and you have a powerhouse of a Ninja!

"Now, what do you think?" "......"

Shikamaru Nara & Temari

Leaf | Sand | Genin | Chunin | Male | Female | Platoon
Mental Power: 5

[STRONG-ARM TACTICS]
During the Exchange of Jutsu, you can discard 2 of your Chakras. In that case, choose one of the following: This Ninja's Team and the Team Battling against this Ninja's Team perform a Mental Power Battle during the turn OR This Ninja's Team and your opponent's Team Battling against this Ninja's Team cannot perform a Mental Power Battle during the turn.

264 © 2002 MASASHI KISHIMOTO

0/3

4/4

PHYSICALLY WEAK? MENTAL THEM OUT!

Mental Power is an alternative way to win battles. When a Mental Power battle is initiated by effects such as the one on Shikamaru Nara & Temari, all Ninjas in the battle that the specific Ninja is in use their Mental Power amounts instead of their normal power. This allows lower-turn Ninjas, such as the incredibly smart Shikamaru Nara, to gain an upper hand on powerful Jonin such as Zabuza Momochi.

NAME: Kakashi Hatake

FIRST APPEARED: *Series 2: Coils of the Snake* (2006)

#18

....

WHY PLAY WITH IT: An obvious powerhouse card, Kakashi Hatake allows you to finish the game faster than usual by dealing direct damage to an opponent, even if Kakashi Hatake becomes blocked. Pairing this effect with 8 Trigram (#8 in our countdown) allows you to get rid of a Ninja permanently!

"How about we put an end to this now?"

Kakashi Hatake 5 1

Leaf | Jonin | Male | Sharingan Eye

[EARLY SETTLEMENT]
Valid: When this Ninja's Team wins a Victory or an Outstanding Victory, you win 1 Battle Reward. When it is Defeated or Completely Defeated, your opponent wins 1 Battle Reward.

3/2

6/3

064   © 2002 MASASHI KISHIMOTO

BINGO BOOK LESSON #1: KAKASHI HATAKE, THE GREAT COPY NINJA!

Age: 26

Sign: Virgo

Birthday: September 15

Rank: Jonin

Teacher: The Fourth Hokage

Hobby: Reading adult-oriented novels

Also known as the Legendary Copy Ninja Kakashi, Kakashi Hatake tends to keep his past to himself. He eventually warms up to Naruto, Sasuke, and Sakura as he becomes the leader of their team, simply known as Team 7.

Though Kakashi is notorious for failing teams straight out of the Academy, Team 7 was the first team he passed, due to their disregard for rules. Seemingly indifferent, Kakashi shows a deep emotional attachment to everyone on his team, proving time and time again that he will sacrifice himself for his students' safety, if the need arises.

Aside from possessing Jonin-level strength, Kakashi's left eye has been imbued with the mystical Uchiha eye technique Sharingan. With this, Kakashi is said to have copied over 1000 Jutsus. A master is not without his weakness, however, and Kakashi is a total sucker for the novels that he constantly reads.

#17

NAME: Secret Wood Style Jutsu:
Deep Forest Creation
FIRST APPEARED: *Series 7:*
Quest for Power (2007)

WHY PLAY WITH IT:
Strong enough to create its own deck-type, this powerful Jutsu has the ability to win the game in a single turn. Though many people think that the card is weak because it can only be used by The First Hokage, others quickly built decks around using this Jutsu consistently, enabling them to win games as soon as the powerful Hokage was on the field!

"So this is the legendary Secret Earth Jutsu of the First Hokage, who brought peace to the land and founded the Hidden Leaf Village!"

Secret Wood Style Jutsu: Deep Forest Creation

土 | 土 | ①

Requirements: "The First Hokage"
Target: Every Ninja of your opponent being sent out to Battle
Effect: The target becomes a Stand-By Ninja. In addition, the target cannot be sent out to Battle during the next turn.

US024 © 2002 MASASHI KISHIMOTO

TURNING OVER A NEW LEAF

The Leaf Village began as the result of an agreement between the Uchiha clan founder and The First Hokage. The village was christened the Leaf Village because of the First Hokage's unique ability to create trees from nothing.

#16

NAME: Lightning Blade
FIRST APPEARED: *Series 9: The Chosen* (2008)

WHY PLAY WITH IT: Another Jutsu card that's just as strong as the previously mentioned Chidori, Lightning Blade has the ability not only to totally remove another Ninja from play but also to allow the remaining two Ninjas to be overpowered by Kakashi, whether he is by himself or in a team!

"By attacking one you infect all. And you don't care. That is not the way of the Shinobi."

Lightning Blade

火 1

Requirements: "Kakashi Hatake"

Target: 1 Ninja Battling against the user

Effect: If your opponent has 5 or more Battle rewards, discard the target. If your opponent has 4 or less Battle rewards, give 1 Damage to the target. Additionally, the user gets +X / + X during this turn. X = the number of your opponent's Battle Rewards.

術 U9066 ✖ © 2002 MASASHI KISHIMOTO • • •

WHY "THE CHOSEN"?

The Chosen was not just full of brand-new cards, it also contained reprints from the first five sets of the Naruto CCG. With so many cards to choose from, members of the forum for Naruto were given 10 spots to choose the top 10 cards they wanted to see in *The Chosen*. And based on player feedback, all ten were reprinted in the set! Want to get involved? With your parent's permission, visit the official Bandai Web site to get started!

NAME: Five-Pronged Seal
FIRST APPEARED: *Series 3: Curse of the Sand*
(2006)

WHY PLAY WITH IT:
Requiring one of each
type of Chakra, this
Jutsu may appear weak
at first, but with all the
ways to draw cards
and build your Chakra
faster, this card quickly
became its own type.
Focusing on getting
rid of your opponent's
hand early in the game,
this card was usually
played by turn 1 with
the assistance of cards
such as Walking on
Water Training and Cliff-
Climbing Training.

"Five-Pronged ... Seal!"

Five-Pronged Seal

雷 火 水 風 土

Target: 1 Ninja Battling against the user
Effect: Return the target and all the cards in your
opponent's hand to their original owner's Deck(s) and
shuffle. If the target is not returned, this effect fails.

衛 092 © 2002 MASASHI KISHIMOTO

#14

NAME: Appearance of Unknown Rivals
FIRST APPEARED: *Series 2: Coils of the Snake*
(2006)

. . . .

WHY PLAY WITH IT: Aside from being an early-game mission, Appearance of Unknown Rivals allows you to draw from zero to three cards total, drawing one every time your opponent plays a Ninja. Your opponent will be forced to play Ninjas in order to keep up with the Ninjas that *you're* playing, so this card guarantees that you will draw at least a few cards from the effect!

BINGO BOOK LESSON #2: ZABUZA MOMOCHI, THE DEMON OF THE CLOUD VILLAGE!

Age: 26

Sign: Leo

Birthday: August 15

Rank: Jonin (Missing Nin)

Association: One of the Seven Swordsmen of the Mist

Hobby: Unknown

Associated with his massive head-cleaving sword, Zabuza is in every way one of the most dangerous people in the Hidden Mist Village. He became a Missing Nin after becoming a Genin through the Hidden Mists twisted testing procedures. Then Zabuza quickly found a right-hand man named Haku and trained him to use his bloodline limit ability in combat. Aside from his large sword, Zabuza is a skillful user of water-type Jutsu, which enables him to cut, capture, or even drown his opponents if the need arises. His favorite technique is his Hidden Mist Jutsu, which enables him to hunt his opponents down by using his keen sense of smell. His opponents are left with zero visibility, leaving them that much more vulnerable to Zabuza.

#13

NAME: Temari
FIRST APPEARED: *Series 6: Eternal Rivalry* (2007)

WHY PLAY WITH IT: Aside from being able to see an opponent's hand at the time she is put into play, Temari can also force your opponent to move one of the Jutsus from his or her hand to your opponent's Chakra area. Add in that she has excellent stats for so early in the game, and you have a staple card that is arguably one of the best turn 1 cards to play!

RELATIONSHIP ADVICE!

Temari is the older sister of both Kankuro and Gaara. Fearing for Gaara's safety numerous times, Temari is very protective of both of them, sometimes risking her own life in order to save theirs!

BAKUGAN

YU-GI-OH!

NARUTO

BELLA SARA

POKÉMON

NAME: Neji Hyuga
FIRST APPEARED: *Series 6: Eternal Rivalry* (2007)

#12

WHY PLAY WITH IT: In addition to having stats that remain unchanged, Neji—true to his Hyuga lineage—can expend some of your Chakra in order to eat through your opponent's Chakra, making it that much harder for your opponent to pull off the large-costing Jutsus. Neji works perfectly in decks that run zero Jutsu and all Missions, as you can then use all of your Chakra to limit your opponent!

BYAKUGAN, ANOTHER EYE TECHNIQUE?

The Hyuga clan's special ability is called Byakugan. Roughly translated as meaning "white eyes," Byakugan gives its user many extra abilities to help in combat, such as being able to see 360 degrees, seeing through objects, and, in some cases (such as Neji) being able to see the Chakra points on someone's body. Utilizing these abilities, the Hyuga clan has developed its own fighting style, dubbed "Gentle Fist." With this style, Neji can cut off an opponent's entire Chakra system, disabling that person's ability to use any Jutsu at all!

#11

NAME: Ino Yamanaka
FIRST APPEARED: *Series 6: Eternal Rivalry* (2007)

WHY PLAY WITH IT: The Yamanaka clan has the special ability to project their souls into other people. Using this card, you can force a Ninja to be sent out to battle as a Head Ninja. This not only accurately reflects Ino's clan ability, but also allows you to control another person's teams!

"Take it away, Choji!"

Ino Yamanaka   0   0

Leaf | Genin | Female | Growth | Mental Power: 1

[FORMATION]
During the Mission Phase, you can select 1 of your opponent's Ninjas. That selected Ninja can only be sent out to Battle as a Head Ninja during the turn.

1/0

0/1   精

us013   © 2002 MASASHI KISHIMOTO

#10

NAME: Just Like Drifting Clouds
FIRST APPEARED: *Series 9: The Chosen* (2008)

WHY PLAY WITH IT:
Fire players have been asking for a long time for a Mission that would allow them to draw cards on the level of other elements. With this Mission, Fire can cycle through its deck efficiently, allowing you to get the cards you need at the time you need them! Just Like Drifting Clouds combines very well with Sakura Haruno (#7 in our countdown).

Designed by Joe Colon (Sannin of 2007)

"Eatin' chips and watchin' clouds... man, this is the best."
"Yep!"

Just Like Drifting Clouds 1 1

Permanent (2)
Effect: During your Mission Phase, you can exchange all the cards in your hand with the same amount of cards from the top of your Deck. In that case, shuffle your Deck and draw 1 card.

作 US086 © 2002 MASASHI KISHIMOTO

PERKS OF BEING ONE OF THE LEGENDARY SANNIN!

Every year, the National-level Sannin tournament for the Naruto CCG is run at GenCon in Indianapolis. The 2007 Sannin winner, Joe Colon, created the Just Like Drifting Clouds card as a prize for winning the Sannin event. Could you be this year's Sannin winner? Get involved in your local organized play for a chance to win such rewards! With your parent's permission, visit the Bandai Web site for more info.

NAME: Water Style: Giant Vortex Jutsu
FIRST APPEARED: *Series 1: Path to Hokage (2006)*

WHY PLAY WITH IT: Surviving gameplay from the very first Naruto set ever released, Giant Vortex Jutsu has been a staple card in Water decks since the beginning of the game. For three Water Chakra, you can return every Ninja battling against the user back to its owner's hand. Cards like Temari and Kabuto can ensure that the Jutsu will not be countered and will thus return your opponent's entire team!

"Water Jutsu: Giant Vortex Jutsu!!!"

Water Style: Giant Vortex Jutsu

水│水│水

Requirements: "Jonin" or higher Rank
Target: Every Ninja Battling against the user
Effect: Move the target back to its original owner's hand.

術 034 © 2002 MASASHI KISHIMOTO

MIX AND MATCH!

See if you can match the Ninja with the village that he or she is a part of.

A) Naruto Uzumaki

1) Hidden Mist Village

B) Zabuza Momochi

2) Hidden Sound Village

C) Kabuto Yakushi

3) Hidden Leaf Village

D) Itachi Uchiha

4) Akatsuki

E) Dosu Kinuta

Answers: A) 3; B) 1; C) 2; D) 4; E) 2

#8

NAME: 8 Trigram Divination Seal Spell Formula

FIRST APPEARED: *Series 1: Path to Hokage* (2006)

WHY PLAY WITH IT: The card that has been repeated the most so far in multiple sets, 8 Trigram is one of Fire's most powerful Jutsus. Comboing and providing powerful synergy with a great number of other cards, any Jonin or higher Ninja can use 8 Trigram, and it only costs two Fire! The best part? It can target *any* Ninja in play, not just the Ninjas battling against you!

"One ninja faced the Nine-Tailed Fox in mortal combat; he sacrificed his life to capture the beast and seal it in a human body."

8 Trigram Divination Seal Spell Formula

火｜火

Requirements: "Jonin" or higher Rank

Target: 1 Ninja

Effect: Move the target back to the top of its original owner's Deck.

術 006 © 2002 MASASHI KISHIMOTO

JUTSU TYPES—NINJA ACADEMY 101!

In the Naruto universe, every Jutsu can be classified into three different types. The first, Ninjutsu, covers the vast majority of Jutsu. Ninjutsu includes Chidori, Rasengan, Water Vortex, and the all-powerful Deep Forest Creation.

The second type, Genjutsu, is a difficult type to master. Genjutsu involves controlling the five senses of the target to display different illusions to that target with the intent to confuse or misdirect. Some very well-known users of Genjutsu include Kakashi Hatake, Kurenai Yuhi, and Itachi Uchiha.

The final type, Taijutsu, are simple techniques that do not require any Chakra at all. These can range from techniques to simple fighting styles, such as Gentle Fist. Rock Lee, once thought to be a worthless Ninja, is a master of Taijutsu and has taken his training to the extreme in an effort to prove his Ninja way: Even without knowing Ninjutsu or Genjutsu, a Ninja can still be great!

NAME: Sakura Haruno
FIRST APPEARED: *Series 6: Eternal Rivalry* (2007)

WHY PLAY WITH IT: Sakura may be a low-stat Ninja to play on your opening turn, but her ability allows you to double your hand size by swapping back and forth with the top of your deck. Paired with cards such as Just Like Drifting Clouds, Sakura can take her effect to the max, allowing you to quickly sift through your deck in a matter of two or three turns!

"A girl's gotta be tough if she's going to survive something like this!"

Sakura Haruno   0   0

Leaf | Genin | Female | Growth | Mental Power: 3

[A DOUBLE PERSONALITY]
During the Exchange of Jutsu, you can exchange all the cards in your hand with the same amount of cards from the top of your Deck.

0/1

SIGNATURE JUTSU BREAKDOWN!

See if you can match the Ninja below to his or her signature Jutsu!

A) Naruto Uzumaki

B) Sasuke Uchiha

C) Rock Lee

D) Ino Yamanaka

E) Shikamaru Nara

F) Choji Akimichi

G) Shino Aburame

H) Neji Hyuga

I) Kiba Inuzuka

1) 8 Trigrams 64 Palms

2) Hidden Lotus

3) Shadow Possession

4) Sexy Jutsu

5) Parasitic Insect Jutsu

6) Fang Over Fang

7) Chidori

8) Expansion Jutsu

9) Mind Transfer Jutsu

#6

NAME: Naruto Uzumaki
FIRST APPEARED: *Series 4: Revenge and Rebirth* (2007)

WHY PLAY WITH IT: Who doesn't want a Jonin-strength Ninja on turn 0? Although it may seem like a steep downside, the effect of this Naruto card guarantees that you keep control of the battle for at least two or three turns. This Naruto can even fight toe-to-toe with Kakashi and tie him in battle! If that isn't enough, you also have all of the Jutsu Naruto can use as well.

NAME: Gaara of the Desert
FIRST APPEARED: *Tin Exclusive* (2007)

WHY PLAY WITH IT: Easily one of the best Gaara cards, this Gaara gives use to your Ninja who you previously thought were useless. By activating his effect, Gaara can "throw" a Ninja at your opponent, dealing 1 damage to one of his or her Ninjas! He even has his own deck-type, which many players have called "Sexy Gaara" due to its ability to use Sexy Jutsu to take your opponent's Ninjas and then throw them back with Gaara's effect. These decks also give heavy emphasis to using Jutsu that anyone could use, such as Paper Bomb or Shadow Clone Jutsu.

#4

NAME: Choji Akimichi
FIRST APPEARED: *Series 6: Eternal Rivalry* (2007)

WHY PLAY WITH IT:
Why not? Choji is a turn 0 that can deal 1 damage to every other turn 0! Although he takes damage at the end of the turn, Choji is still a formidable Ninja, especially when Ino forces a Ninja to the front of the battle and Shikamaru shuts it down. Now that's teamwork!

"My pleasure!"

Choji Akimichi 0

Leaf | Genin | Male | Growth

[FORMATION]
When this Ninja is sent out to Battle and opposed, you can give 1 Damage to 1 of your opponent's Ninjas Battling agaist this Ninja with 0 Entrance cost. In that case, give 1 Damage to this Ninja at the end of the turn.

0/0

2/0

US016 © 2002 MASASHI KISHIMOTO

INO-SHIKA-CHO: THE SECRET TO THE COMBO!

Throughout the generations of the Leaf Village, the members of the Akimichi, Yamanaka, and Nara clans have always had great synergy with one another. It is no different today with Ino, Shikamaru, and Choji. Shikamaru captures the target with his Shadow Possession technique, causing the target to stand still. Ino can then mentally transfer her soul into the target's body at this point, or Choji can use his powerful Expansion Jutsu to do some massive damage to the target!

#3

NAME: Naruto vs. Sasuke
FIRST APPEARED: *Waterfall Ninja* movie
(promo card) (2007)

WHY PLAY IT: Naruto vs. Sasuke pits your Genins against your opponent's Genins. If you build a deck around it, such as using Choji Akimichi, Gaara of the Desert, and Naruto Uzumaki, you are nearly guaranteed to have stronger Genin and will win all the fights!

NAME: Gaara of the Desert
FIRST APPEARED: *Series 8: Battle of Destiny* (2008)

WHY PLAY WITH IT:
Based on the popular Internet phenomenon, many people quickly built a deck around this Gaara and called the deck "Over 9000" or >9k for short, due to Gaara's "Immense Power." Pairing this card with Gaara's Jutsus, such as Sand Tomb, Double Sand Blade, and even Sand Coffin allows you to continuously search your deck for his Jutsus, pulling them out to deal with any situation that might present itself!

"It's extremely simple for me to generate sand out of soil."

Gaara of the Desert

Sand | Genin | Male

[IMMENSE POWER]
When this Ninja is sent out to Battle, you can search for 1 Jutsu card with "Requirements: "Sand" Combat Attribute" in the top 5 cards of your Deck, show it to your opponent, and place it in your hand. Then, return the rest to the top of your Deck and shuffle it.

295 © 2002 MASASHI KISHIMOTO

NAME: Shikamaru Nara

FIRST APPEARED: *Series 6: Eternal Rivalry* (2007)

WHY PLAY WITH IT: Shikamaru Nara is above and beyond the best card ever printed in the Naruto game so far. He has the best statistics for turn 1, best characteristics, and one of the best effects ever. Not only does he work with Choji and Ino, he also works with other cards that refer to turn cost, such as The First Hokage. His secondary effect is what's really best, though. Being able to negate any effect on the board from any Ninja puts him on the highest pedestal above and beyond everyone else in the game. His only downfall is his non-valid ability and his 0/0 injured stats, but these are nothing compared to what he can do for your game!

"I'll leave the girl to you."

Shikamaru Nara

Leaf | Genín | Male | Growth | Mental Power: 4

[FORMATION]

While this Ninja is Battling, the Entrance cost of the Head Ninja Battling against this Ninja's Team becomes 0 and it's effect text is negated.

0/0

0/2

us014 © 2002 MASASHI KISHIMOTO

DUELISTS: MONSTERS AWAIT YOU IN THE YU-GI-OH! TRADING CARD GAME

With Spells and Traps to either support your monsters or defeat your opponent's monsters, the Yu-Gi-Oh! Trading Card Game is an exciting, pitched battle between two players—or Duelists—who try to bring each other's Life Points down to 0. You'll need powerful attacks, strong defenses, and clever tricks to defeat the incredibly powerful Warriors, Dragons, and Beasts you'll encounter when you play!

Based on the card game from the *Yu-Gi-Oh!* TV series and *Yu-Gi-Oh! GX* comic, the Yu-Gi-Oh Trading Card Game gives you thousands of cards to choose from to build your 40-card deck. Since the game came to the U.S. from Japan in 2002 with the *Legend of Blue Eyes White Dragon* release, Duelists have had lots of different ways to collect the cards they want to use in battle: booster packs, Starter Decks, Structure Decks, tins, and promo cards.

What do you need to start Dueling? Starter decks (which are named after characters from the TV show) are a great place to begin. Once you've learned the basics, you'll be ready to move up to Structure Decks. These are a little harder to master, but they have cool themes and strong card combos.

Then you'll be ready to start building decks on your own to compete in leagues, Shonen Jump's Championship, Nationals, and maybe even the Yu-Gi-Oh! World Championships!

LET'S DUEL!

In the Yu-Gi-Oh! Trading Card Game, you and your opponent each have a deck of 40 cards. In that deck are all the monsters, Spell cards, and Trap cards you will need to Duel, or battle.

(You also might decide to have a separate Extra Deck—formerly called the Fusion Deck—with some additional monsters in it and a Side Deck with extra cards to rotate in and out of your Main Deck.)

Each of you draws cards, and it's time for the player who goes first to begin!

On your turn, you'll 1) Summon monsters in a variety of ways, 2) Set Spell and Trap Cards to use against your opponent later on, 3) activate Spells and Traps that you Set earlier, and 4) get your monsters ready to Duel by changing their position between Attack and Defense. And, of course, you'll Duel!

Sometimes your monsters will need to attack your opponent's monsters. When that happens, you'll first look at the position of your opponent's monster to see if it's in Attack or Defense position. Then you'll compare your Attack (ATK) Points to either its ATK or its Defense (DEF) Points, and then you'll do damage back and forth to see who wins the Duel. Sometimes, all your opponent's monsters will be destroyed and sent to the Graveyard—that's when you'll get to attack *your opponent* to try to take away Life Points!

You each start the game with 8000 Life Points. When you attack and bring your opponent's Life Points down to 0, you win!

Try out a Starter Deck to play the first time—it'll give you all you need to start on the path of becoming an expert Duelist!

#25

NAME: Uria, Lord of Searing Flames
SET: *Shadow of Infinity* booster packs (2006)

IT'S COOL BECAUSE: The 10 stars just below this Pyro monster's name (which tell you it's a Level 10) are your first clue to just how powerful it is. In order to get it into play, you need to give up three of your own Trap Cards. Though this is a little hard to do, it's well worth it when Uria gets at least 3000 ATK from the Trap Cards you just put in your Graveyard, which is quite impressive!

SPRINGING TRAPS

Trap Cards can cause you all sorts of problems if they're not your own! They're often facedown on your opponent's side, waiting for you to attack before springing to disrupt your game. So, use them to your advantage while trying to get Uria into play—use Trap Cards like Gravity Bind (from *Dark Beginning 1*) to hold your opponent's attacks off for a bit. Once Uria is in your Monster Zone, you can start destroying any and all Trap or Spell Cards your opponent might be saving to surprise you with!

NAME: Elemental Hero Shining Flare Wingman
SET: *Elemental Energy* booster packs (2005)

IT'S COOL BECAUSE: It can be very difficult to get this E-Hero into play because of its high cost. First, you need to get Elemental Hero Avian and Elemental Hero Burstinatrix into your hand or into play so you can Fusion Summon Elemental Hero Flame Wingman. Then you need Elemental Hero Sparkman to combine with your Elemental Hero Flame Wingman to finally Fusion Summon Elemental Hero Shining Flare Wingman! (Cards like Future Fusion will make this a little easier for you.) And once you get it into play, it's super-powerful, with a likely 3700 ATK! That's a great monster to have on your side!

FUSION CONFUSION?

Fusion Monsters are special monsters from a separate deck, your Extra Deck. (This is where you'll also have Synchro Monsters, if you decide to use them.) You don't need an Extra Deck to play, but having one lets you get powerful monsters into play by combining and destroying smaller monsters in exchange. A Fusion Summons requires you to use the card Polymerization to bring that monster into play, but there are sometimes other ways to get those monsters from your Extra Deck. (And Synchro Monsters only need a Tuner Monster!)

#23

NAME: Destiny Draw
SET: *Aster Phoenix* Duelist Packs (2007)

IT'S COOL BECAUSE:
Some cards only work in certain types of decks, and Destiny Draw is one of those. But in the right deck—one with lots of Destiny Hero cards in it—it gives you a great advantage in trying to get to just the right cards you need to win.

DECK-BUILDING DESTINY!

Many decks are built around certain themes or card concepts. Destiny Draw is very popular in decks nicknamed "Diamond Dude Turbo" (or "DDT"), which are built around Destiny Hero–Diamond Dude, Destiny Hero–Malicious, and a handful of other cards to make it a fast, aggressive deck!

NAME: Vennominaga The Deity of Poisonous Snakes

SET: *Tactical Evolution* booster packs (2007)

IT'S COOL BECAUSE: Getting Vennominaga into play is challenging (it's how it works for most of the best cards) because it's a tricky combination of Vennominon the King of Poisonous Snakes and the Trap Card Rise of the Snake Deity. But once you have Vennominaga in play, you could easily be just three turns away from victory, thanks to its Hyper-Venom attack. It also helps that almost the only way your opponent can get rid of it is through battle, since it can't be targeted and is safe from the effects of monsters, Spells, and Traps!

WHAT'S THE NAGA WITH YOU?

The name "Vennominaga" ends with the term used in Hindu and Buddhism for a race of divine beings that take the shape of snake-people, the Naga.

TAKIN' TOKENS!

Use Ojama Trio to put three Ojama Tokens in Defense Position on your opponent's side of the field (they each have 1000 Defense Points when you do). Then use Final Attack Orders to put them in Attack Position. When you attack one of them each turn, you'll destroy them and still do damage to your opponent—which is just what you need to do to get a Hyper-Venom Counter on Vennominaga!

#21

NAME: Allure of Darkness
SET: *Phantom Darkness* booster packs (2008)

IT'S COOL BECAUSE: Allure of Darkness is another powerful card that lets you draw cards at the cost of removing from play a Dark monster from your hand. Removing from play is different than discarding it to your Graveyard, but Trap Cards like Escape from the Dark Dimension will let you bring back that Dark monster, much to your opponent's surprise! And if you have no cards in your hand at all, you can still use Allure of Darkness to draw two cards . . . and discard your entire hand as the penalty for not discarding a Dark monster. Of course, since you don't have any cards in your hand, that was drawing two cards for free!

FORBIDDEN, LIMITED, AND SEMI-LIMITED

Some cards are just too powerful for their own good. So, while you can build decks with three copies of some very powerful cards in them, in certain tournament or other competitions, you might only be allowed one, two, or even none of some cards! Allure of Darkness, for example, is Semi-Limited—you can only put two Allure of Darkness cards in your 40-card deck. Chaos Emperor Dragon, on the other hand, is so powerful that it's on the Forbidden list in the Advanced format! The lists change from time to time; you can find them at the official Yu-Gi-Oh! Web site, go to your country, and check under "Game Play" for Forbidden/Limited Cards! Be sure to get your parent's permission.

#20

NAME: Neo-Spacian Grand Mole
SET: *Strike of Neos* booster packs (2007)

IT'S COOL BECAUSE: Neo-Spacian Grand Mole has the unusual history of being Restricted to one per deck even before it was ready to be added to tournament decks. More than anything, it's meant to be a serious annoyance to your opponent. If your opponent has played a huge monster that took a lot of effort to get into play—a big Tribute, a difficult Fusion—then Neo-Spacian Grand Mole simply sends it back to his or her hand to start all over again. Plus, it can clear a path for you to attack your opponent's Life Points.

NEO-SPACIAN GRAND MOLE

STON-EN005

[ROCK / EFFECT]
If this card attacks or is attacked by an opponent's monster, you can return both monsters to their owners' hands at the start of the Damage Step (without damage calculation).

ATK/ 900 DEF/ 300

80344569   ©1996 KAZUKI TAKAHASHI

MOLE RARE . . . OR MOLE ULTRA RARE?

Neo-Spacian Grand Mole comes in two different versions in the *Strike of Neos* boosters—Rare and Ultimate Rare. But what's the difference? Well, Rare cards have their name printed in silver foil; Ultimate Rare cards have gold foil lettering and embossed holographic art. (There are also Parallel Rares, Secret Rares, Super Rares, and Ultra Rares.) Between the two versions of Neo-Spacian Grand Mole, you can probably guess which one is more valuable and harder to get!

- Common

- Short Print Common

- Super Short Print Common

- Rare (common cards with names in silver foil)

- Super Rare (holographic art)

- Ultra Rare (names in gold foil, foil art)

- Secret Rare (names in silver foil, glossy, sparkling holographic art)

- Ultimate Rare (names in gold foil, foil art, embossed or "raised" art)

- Parallel Rare (names in gold foil, entire card is shiny)

NAME: Card Trooper
#19 **SET:** *Jaden Yuki 2* Duelist Packs (2007)

IT'S COOL BECAUSE: Most monsters with 1900 ATK are *not* going to be Level 3, so they're going to cost you more. Card Trooper not only gains power based on your needs, it also lets you get cards into your Graveyard faster. This can be a benefit—see Dark Armed Dragon, for instance. Then Card Trooper is good enough to reward you with a card to your hand when it goes to the Graveyard itself. (Oh, and it's Limited in tournament formats, meaning you can only have one copy of it in your deck.) Still . . . Is that a trooper, or what?

CARD TROOPER

[MACHINE / EFFECT]
Once per turn, you can send up to 3 cards from the top of your Deck to the Graveyard. This card gains 500 ATK for each card sent to the Graveyard this way, until the end of this turn. When this card on your side of the field is destroyed and sent to your Graveyard, draw 1 card.

ATK/ 400 DEF/ 400

DIGGING UP A WINNER

Magical Stone Excavation (from the *2006 Champion Pack Game Two*) was in so many expert-level decks for a reason: it lets you get rid of a couple of cards from your hand that you can do without in exchange for a Spell card that you *really* need back! It has a few drawbacks, though. The card itself is still expensive to buy. Plus, you need to have a real use for it to get the most out of it. And even though you can only have two copies of it in your deck in tournaments, it's still a fan favorite!

UPPER DECK'S UPPER HAND

Both Card Trooper and Magical Stone were the central cards in an April Fool's letter sent from Upper Deck to judges. The letter told them how both cards had been terribly mistranslated and gave them the "correct" card text for each card. If it was true, that would have made lots of past tournaments turn out very differently! But by reading the first letter of each sentence in the letter, you could see the words "A-P-R-I-L-F-O-O-L-S" spelled out!

NAME: Cyber Dragon
#18
SET: *Cybernetic Revolution* booster packs (2005)

IT'S COOL BECAUSE: For a long time, Cyber Dragon was THE card in all the most successful decks. With so many cards being added to the game regularly, Cyber Dragon still hasn't lost its usefulness (though it is now Semi-Limited to two copies in your deck). It can get into play without paying any Tribute if your opponent has even 1 monster and you don't have any. It comes in with enough ATK Points to do some serious damage in a hurry. Plus, it has appeared in a number of different products now (like a 2006 Collector's Tin), so you shouldn't have any trouble finding this great dragon to add to your deck!

CYBER TRICKS!

Some players first bring Cyber Dragon into play when they have no monsters. After that, they immediately use Cyber Dragon as Tribute to bring in something with other useful effects, like Jinzo (which shuts down Trap Cards)!

TRIVIA

The Cyber Dragon is supposedly based on the dragon from which country?

Answer: China.

NAME: Crystal Beast Ruby Carbuncle
SET: *Force of the Breaker* booster packs (2007)

IT'S COOL BECAUSE: Aside from being probably the cutest card on this whole list, Crystal Beast Ruby Carbuncle is perfect for a deck built specially around Crystal Beasts. It might not be terribly strong, but you don't really need it for its fighting ability. Instead, you need it so you can bring as many other Crystal Beast cards from your Spell and Trap Zone as possible! Try it with other Crystal Beast cards—the Amber Mammoth lets you redirect your opponent's attacks, for instance. Plus, Crystal Beast Ruby Carbuncle recycles back to the Spell and Trap Zone instead of going to the Graveyard!

SWARM!

Use Crystal Promise or Crystal Beacon to Special Summon Ruby Carbuncle when your Spell and Trap Zone is as full as it can be with Crystal Beast cards. Then let the fun begin when they all come out to attack at once!

117

BAKUGAN

YU-GI-OH!

NARUTO

BELLA SARA

POKÉMON

#16

NAME: Judgment Dragon
SET: *Light of Destruction* booster packs (2008)

IT'S COOL BECAUSE: A newcomer to the Dueling scene, Judgment Dragon is the Light to Dark Armed Dragon's . . . uh, Dark! Judgment Dragon's Special Summon requirement of four different Lightsworn monsters in your Graveyard is actually not so hard—the Lightsworn monsters are good at moving cards all over the place. Then you can give up 1000 of your Life Points in order to clear all the other cards off the field and attack for 3000 of your opponent's Life Points. A great trade! With this kind of power, could Judgment Dragon end up being Limited or even Forbidden? Not yet!

PASSING JUDGMENT

While sending four cards every turn from your Deck to your Graveyard to keep Judgment Dragon in play, keep your eyes open for Wulf, Lightsworn Beast to go by. It can be Special Summoned from your Graveyard into play to help Judgment Dragon win the Duel for you!

#15

NAME: Skyscraper 2–Hero City
SET: *Strike of Neos* booster packs (2007)

IT'S COOL BECAUSE: For a while, Skyscraper 2–Hero City appeared in a specific deck type nicknamed "Big City." Being able to bring Elemental Heroes that were destroyed back to the field can keep your deck moving quickly, and some Heroes are well worth bringing back!

Use this with Elemental Hero Stratos (Stratos lets you either destroy Spell or Trap Cards in the field when it comes back this way or add an Elemental Hero, Destiny Hero, or Evil Hero from your Deck to your hand). Or try Skscraper 2–Hero City with Elemental Hero Ocean. (Ocean lets you return an Elemental Hero or Destiny Hero to your hand from the field or the Graveyard.)

FIELD SPELLS!

Like Skyscraper 2–Hero City, Necrovalley and Rainbow Ruin affect the entire field, hopefully to your advantage! Necrovalley will keep your opponents from playing all those cards that let them use their Graveyards as a valuable resource. Ancient City–Rainbow Ruins (which is as good as Skyscraper 2–Hero City) is a spectacular resource for Crystal Beast decks, building in power with every additional Crystal Beast you have in play!

NAME: Dark Magician of Chaos
SET: *Dark Revelation 2* booster packs (2005)

IT'S COOL BECAUSE: Want to stop your opponent from filling up his or her Graveyard with all the useful cards to win? First, Special Summon Dark Magician of Chaos using Monster Reborn when it's in your Graveyard. When it comes into play, you can get the Monster Reborn Spell Card back into your hand or you get another heavy-hitter Spell Card that could win you the game! Plus, with 2800 ATK and a 2600 DEF, Dark Magician of Chaos will win most battles, sending your opponent's monsters out of play instead of to the Graveyard. When Dark Magician leaves play, you can always use Dimension Fusion or Escape from the Dark Dimension to get it back!

GET THE DARK PARTY STARTED!

To get Dark Magician of Chaos into play a bit faster, try using Foolish Burial to get it right from your Deck into your Graveyard. There, it'll be ready for you to use Monster Reborn to bring it into the field!

NAME: Mirror Force
SET: *Dark Beginning 2* booster packs (2005)

IT'S COOL BECAUSE: It's so simple: if one of your opponent's monsters attacks, you spring the trap Mirror Force, and all of your opponent's monsters that are in the Attack Position are destroyed. It's Limited, so you can have only one in your deck, but that might be all you need . . .

GET THEM FIRST!

You can collect four Yu-Gi-Oh! Trading Card Game releases every year. Most of them are released as First Edition cards, which, if you are collecting them for their value, are worth almost double what the follow-up Unlimited (non-First Edition) cards are worth. You can also collect special releases in Collector Tins, Duelist Packs, Tournament Series, Champion Packs, and lots of promo cards. (In 2002, you could even get Yu-Gi-Oh! promo cards at McDonald's®!)

#12

NAME: Crystal Beast Sapphire Pegasus
SET: *Force of the Breaker* booster packs (2007)

IT'S COOL BECAUSE: To make any deck built around Crystal Beasts, the Sapphire Pegasus is an absolute necessity. Use Crystal Beacon or Crystal Promise to get it into play faster. Most experienced Duelists would suggest that you put three of them in your Crystal deck to be sure you get this important card when you need it!

IN SEARCH OF THE PEGASUS

The Crystal Beast Sapphire Pegasus appears in the artwork on Crystal Blessing (*Force of the Breake*r), Crystal Pair (*Jesse Anderson* Duelist Packs), and on two cards that have only been released in Japanese so far: Golden Rule and Gem Fortress, which shows all seven Crystal Beasts on one card.

NAME: Cyber End Dragon
SET: *Cybernetic Revolution* booster packs (2005)

IT'S COOL BECAUSE: For sheer ATK power, nothing beats this Fusion Monster. 4000! What makes it especially dangerous is that, as a rule, you don't do any Battle Damage to your opponent when your attacking monster's ATK is higher than his or her monster's DEF; you just destroy your opponent's monster. Cyber End Dragon not only sends your opponent's monster to the Graveyard, it also sends any damage that's left over right onto your opponent. Get this out early in the game, and you are almost assured victory!

CYBER END SUPERSIZE?

Two Limited Cards will help you make Cyber End Dragon even more dangerous when the time to attack comes. First, Limiter Removal doubles Cyber End Dragon's ATK for one turn (but sends it to the Graveyard at the end of that turn). Then Megamorph doubles its ATK as long as you have lower Life Points than your opponent . . . which won't be for long!

NAME: Golden Sarcophagus
SET: Shonen Jump Championship Series
Prize Card (2007)

IT'S COOL BECAUSE: Gold Sarcophagus is Limited to one in your deck, but you're not likely to have more than one anyway! It guarantees you any card you need from your deck in just two turns, no matter what happens to Golden Sarcophagus. Given out as a prize card in touring Shonen Jump Championship Series events, Golden Sarcophagus doesn't appear in any sets yet, so it's still hard to come by. But if you can get it, it belongs in any deck you build!

SARCOPHAGUS OF A DIFFERENT SORT

Different Dimension Capsule has an effect similar to Golden Sarcophagus, the biggest difference being that your opponent can't stop the Sarcophagus. Different Dimension Capsule will be a target from the moment you play it to keep you from getting that card you want!

#9

NAME: Dark Armed Dragon
SET: *Phantom Darkness* booster packs (2008)

IT'S COOL BECAUSE: With 2800 Attack Points, Dark Armed Dragon is already a huge threat to your opponents. That's a lot of damage for them to risk taking! But even better is the requirement to Special Summon Dark Armed Dragon into play—you need to have exactly three Dark monsters in your Graveyard. If you've got that taken care of, Dark Armed Dragon comes onto the field . . . and proceeds to get rid of anything annoying on your opponent's side of the field! You'll get rid of at least three cards on your opponent's side (since you have three Dark monsters in your Graveyard already), and that might be enough to end the game in your favor in a hurry!

SAY GOOD KNIGHT TO YOUR OPPONENTS . . .

Not exactly sure how to control the number of Dark monsters in your Graveyard so you can get Dark Armed Dragon into play? Well, Armageddon Knight lets you put a Dark monster from your Deck to your Graveyard when the Knight comes into play. Or try Dark Grepher—it can get all three Dark monsters into your Graveyard all by itself in no time!

#8

NAME: Monster Reborn
SET: *Dark Beginning 1* booster packs (2004)

IT'S COOL BECAUSE: It's been easy to find in numerous starter decks, and it's been Limited to one per deck for awhile. It's simple to use and works great with any cards that let you put cards in your Graveyard (like Judgment Dragon). After you've used it, you can get it back and use it again with cards like Magician of Faith or Magical Stone Excavation. You'll feel reborn the first time you use Monster Reborn to bring back the game-winning power monster!

ᗞIᗞ YOU KNOW . . . ?

. . . that the artwork for Monster Reborn was changed between the Japanese and the English versions? The Japanese version featured an ankh, an Egyptian hieroglyphic that means "life," and it is considered by many to be a religious symbol.

YOU-SHOULD-GO...
TO THE WEB SITES!

Yu-Gi-Oh! Web sites are great places to learn more about the game, the individual cards, and the strategies that can help you become an even better Duelist! There are many fan sites where you can get all sorts of advice and guidance from players of all skill levels. And of course, the official Yu-Gi-Oh! site will get you started with an overview of the entire game and one of the best online demos for a game you'll find anywhere! Be sure to get your parent's permission to check out these sites.

#7

NAME: Torrential Tribute
SET: *Dark Beginning 1* booster packs (2004)

IT'S COOL BECAUSE: The simplest effects are sometimes the best, and in the case of Torrential Tribute, any deck you play will benefit from it. You can use it when your opponent Summons a monster or, if you have another plan, you can activate it when you Summon one of your own monsters! Timing is important with this Limited card, but with some monsters unable to be destroyed in battle, Torrential Tribute is a necessity to clear the field.

WHAT COMES AFTER THE TORRENT?

Once there are no monsters on the field, it's time to get one into play on your side quickly. Play monsters from your hand, or try using Premature Burial or Call of the Haunted to get a surprise advantage over your monster-less opponent!

NAME: Heavy Storm
SET: *Dark Beginning 2* booster packs (2005)

IT'S COOL BECAUSE: After you've destroyed all those monsters with Torrential Tribute, why not go for all the Spell and Trap Cards in play, too?

HEAVY STORM

[SPELL CARD]

KONAMI

1st Edition   SD2-EN019

Destroy all Spell and Trap Cards on the field.

19613556   ©1996 KAZUKI TAKAHASHI

MORE HEAVY HITTERS

Besides Torrential Tribute and Heavy Storm, there are a few other classic cards that cause mass destruction. Try Dark Hole (from *Dark Beginning 1*), which does basically the same thing as Torrential Tribute . . . without the Summoning restriction. Or check out Harpie's Feather Duster (from *Tournament Series 8*), which destroys all of your opponent's Spell and Trap Cards. Finally, Raigeki (from *Dark Beginning 1*) destroys all monsters on your opponent's side of the field. All three of these cards, however, are on the Forbidden List, making Torrential Tribute and Heavy Storm your best bets!

NAME: Raiza the Storm Monarch
SET: *Force of the Breaker* booster packs (2007)

IT'S COOL BECAUSE: The only Limited Monarch, Raiza the Storm Monarch comes with a lot of choices—what card will you send back to the top of your opponent's deck to clear a path to attack (which is even cooler if that card was a hard one to get into play the first time!) or to stop a Spell or Trap that's been worrying you? Best of all, you know what your opponent is going to draw on his or her next turn, which gives you yet another immediate card advantage!

A TRIBUTE TO THE LEVEL OF PLAY

Monsters that are Level 5 or Level 6—that is, ones that have five or six stars below their name—require you to put another monster into your Graveyard as a cost of putting that Level 5 or 6 monster on the field. And monsters that are Level 7 or higher require 2 Tributes, so it can be hard to get a big monster into play . . . unless it has a cost like Dark Armed Dragon, where you have to meet other conditions to bring it in!

LET YOUR OPPONENT'S MONSTERS BOW DOWN!

Raiza the Storm Monarch deserves the royal treatment when it comes to Tributes. So, use Soul Exchange or the Limited Brain Control to take over one of your *opponent's* monsters long enough to use it for Tribute to Raiza, clearing yet another obstacle when you attack!

BY ANY OTHER TITLE

Raiza's name is spelled the same, but can you match the translations of "The Storm Monarch" to their languages?

A) Monarque de la Tempête   1) Spanish

B) Der Sturmmonarch   2) German

C) Il Monarca della Tempesta   3) French

D) El Monarca de las Tormentas   4) Italian

Answers: A) 3; B) 2; C) 4; D) 1

NAME: Sangan
SET: *Dark Beginning 2* booster packs (2005)

IT'S COOL BECAUSE: You might hear the word "tutor" used to describe Sangan's effect of searching your deck for a card and putting it into your hand. It's a term that began with the trading card game *Magic: The Gathering* to describe this very act. Sangan is Limited, but that one card could make a big difference to you, and Sangan is small enough when in play that your opponent will have a hard time deciding whether to use a Trap Card on it or not. After all, many Traps will send Sangan to the Graveyard, which is why you want to play it in the first place!

PICK ME, PICK ME!

When it's time to use Sangan's effect, choose wisely—you want monsters that will continue the benefits for your side. Exiled Force, for instance, has an ATK less than 1500 and you can Tribute it to destroy one of your opponent's monsters!

NAME: Gladiator Beast Gyzarus
SET: *Light of Destruction* booster packs (2008)

IT'S COOL BECAUSE: A cornerstone of Gladiator Beast decks, Gyzarus has a great effect when it comes into play by destroying up to two cards on the field. Because it says "up to," Gyzarus doesn't have to destroy itself or any of *your* cards if your opponent has an empty field. And by being able to disappear back into your Extra Deck in exchange for two Gladiator Beast monsters from your Deck, Gladiator Beast Gyzarus creates opportunities for you to catch your opponent off guard.

ACE YOUR TEST!

Worried that you won't be able to find that Gladiator Beast Bestiari when you need it to get Gladiator Beast Gyzarus out of your Extra Deck? Test Tiger will solve that problem for you by allowing you to trade a Gladiator Beast from your Monster Zone for one in your deck—in this case, Gladiator Beast Bestiari!

NAME OF THE BEAST

"Gyzarus" comes from the word "Kaiser," the German word based on the name Caesar and meaning "emperor."

NAME: Light and Darkness Dragon
SET: *Light and Darkness* Power Pack (2007)

IT'S COOL BECAUSE: Once you pay the two-monster Tribute to get Light and Darkness Dragon into play, you effectively shut down multiple effects from Traps, Spells, and Effect Monsters every single turn, assuming your Dragon doesn't get destroyed. For a time, the game will just be about battling! And once Light and Darkness Dragon is destroyed, you're still going to get a monster back from your Graveyard at the cost of losing all the other cards you control. Many expert decks (including Japanese decks that went all the way to the World Championships) made good use of this card, watching carefully for cards like Treeborn Frog that could frustrate it!

SO GOOD . . .

Light and Darkness Dragon was so good that it was promptly made Semi-Limited (meaning you can have only two in your Deck). It was released as part of a special Light and Darkness Power Pack that included the Dragon plus two 12-card *Dark Revelation 4* booster packs and a 32-page manga sample of *Yu-Gi-Oh! GX* that tells the story of the Light and Darkness Dragon!

HONORABLE MENTION: YATA-GARASU

From the 2005 *Dark Beginning 2* release, it's on the Forbidden List (which means it's not allowed in any official tournaments or competitions), but it's the one Forbidden card that most older players have an opinion about. With other card combinations that emptied your opponent's hand and cleared the field of your opponent's monsters, Yata-Garasu could be set for a "Yata-Lock." This means your opponent would be helpless to stop you from winning, no matter how many turns it took you. Every time your opponent is not allowed to draw a card because of Yata-Garasu, you just get that much more ahead. It's easy to see why it was Forbidden!

ORGANIZED PLAY

Most cards on the Yu-Gi-Oh! Forbidden List are extremely powerful, so much so that they could easily form a whole separate list of 25 great cards! But you can't play with them anywhere but in casual play, so they've been left off of this list. So, if you're going to skip most Forbidden cards, where will you play your deck? Many local game stores have tournaments, and the makers of the game—Upper Deck, Konami, and Shonen Jump—all have systems in their regions to host tournaments with cool prizes. Most tournaments use the "Advanced Format," which has rules about Forbidden and Limited cards, so be sure to check the lists when you're ready to build and compete.

NAME: Crush Card Virus
SET: *Gold Series* (2008)

IT'S COOL BECAUSE: Before it was a crazy-valuable card from the Gold Series (costing hundreds of dollars), Crush Card Virus was only available as an even crazier-valuable card as a Shonen Jump Championship Series Prize Card (costing *thousands* of dollars). Many popular decks often count on their bigger monsters to win the game. That's what Crush Card Virus will stop for three whole turns! The monster most logical to Tribute for this is Sangan (see #12), and the control it gives you over all of your opponent's cards will make the rewards from Sangan that much sweeter!

CRUSH CARD TRIVIA!

The Japanese symbol on the card, the Kanji *shi*, means "death," which is appropriate since the name of the card in Japanese means "Deck Destruction Virus of Death." And if you like Crush Card Virus, be sure to check out Deck Devastation Virus!

ANSWER THE CALL IN BAKUGAN BATTLE BRAWLERS!

Trading card games roll in a whole new direction in Bakugan Battle Brawlers. Bakugan combines trading cards with marbles that morph into unique creatures called Bakugan. The cards both trigger the morphing and add new dimensions to every battle. Since its U.S. release in early 2008, Bakugan has become incredibly popular.

In addition to the trading card game, Bakugan—which is Japanese for "exploding sphere"—has branched out into a wide variety of other areas, including a show on Cartoon Network® that helps to explain the world of the game. When children in our world discover these unique cards and begin to play battle games with them, similar battles are also happening in another dimension called Vestroia, where Bakugan warriors face one another in combat. Some of them are trapped in field cards and sent to Earth, which is where our hero Dan and his friends discover them and begin their battle to save both dimensions.

There are many different Bakugan to choose from, some of which are already very valuable and have even been "retired" to make room for new brawlers. There are also new products to help make your games even easier—launchers to send your Bakugan rolling out onto the field, Battle Arenas to give you a perfect field for combat, and Starter Packs to get you right into the battles!

You can learn to play in just minutes, and then you'll be ready to answer the call to brawl . . . and decide the fate of the galaxy!

LET'S BRAWL!

To play Bakugan Battle Brawlers, all you need are at least three Bakugan, three Gate cards, and three Ability cards. Once you and your opponent each have these, you're ready to start rolling!

Each of you will take turns placing Gate cards on the field. Gate cards are heavier because they have special triggers inside to make Bakugan pop open. Once your Gate cards are set, you'll take turns rolling your unused Bakugan onto the field. Your goal is to land on a Gate card that will make your Bakugan burst out of it sphere, ready to battle.

When your Bakugan and your opponent's Bakugan both open up on the same Gate card, it's time to fight for control! You'll flip over the Gate card to see how it affects each Bakugan's G Powers (a special number written on every Bakugan), and then you and your opponent might play Ability cards to change those numbers up or down. The highest number wins, and the more powerful Bakugan takes the Gate card!

Once there are no Bakugan remaining or all the cards have been won, the game is over. Players add up the values of their Gate cards

and bonuses for Bakugan they won or didn't use. The player with the hightest score wins!

Everything you need to play is in a Starter Pack. For more choices, try a Battle Pack, which gives you six Bakugan, six Ability cards, and Six Gate cards!

You can see a great demo of the game—as well as lots of information about the cards, the universe, playing with more than two players, and, of course, Bakugan themselves—at the official Bakugan Web site! Be sure to get your parent's permission to visit the site.

Bakugan Battle Brawlers isn't just cards—it's cards *and* Bakugan. You'll need both to do battle, so check out ten of the coolest cards that will help your strategies *and* ten of the coolest Bakugan that will win your games for you!

#10 BAKUGAN: Darkus Serpenoid

A GREAT BRAWLER BECAUSE: Darkus Bakugan are among the most dangerous, and the snakelike Serpenoids are

powerful because of their association with Naga, the evil one who possesses the Silent Core. Many players favor Darkus Bakugan because of the bonuses they sometimes get on Gate cards!

CARD: Dusk

POWERFUL BECAUSE: Many cards are meant to support the Bakugan you decide to battle with. The rare card Dusk strongly supports your Darkus Bakugan by giving them a huge boost to their G-Power when you finally get to brawling—140 extra points! Each of the types of Bakugan has a unique card that helps it—like Fire Pit for Pyrus Bakugan or Whirlpool for Aquos Bakugan. Build your arsenal with these kinds of cards in mind!

DUSK

80
20
20
60
140
120

BA137-GA-SM Bakugan™ 2008 Spin Masters LTD. & SEGA Toys 5/48

ROLL OUT THE CARDS!

The cards you choose before battle can both slow down your opponent and give you that extra boost you need to win.

Normal cards are the simplest—they're Gate cards that boost everyone's Bakugan in battle (see #3, for example). Like all cards, Normal cards have an HSP score—this is the number of points you'll get at the end of the game if you win the battle and take this card as your prize!

Character cards give one particular kind of Bakugan a huge boost, usually by doubling its G-Power (see #9).

Command cards (see #8) bring the element of surprise to your battles and might change the outcome of a battle, one way or another.

Special Ability cards are cards that you can only play once in a game. If you play a Special Ability card at just the right time, it can give you great benefits in a battle!

DAN'S THROW

Play before you roll. If this roll results in a battle, you may take back one of your Ability cards from your used pile.

Joue avant de lancer. S'il y a bataille lors de cette manche, tu pourras reprendre une de es cartes Capacités de la pile "Hors Jeu".

BA162-AB-SM-GBL Bakugan™ 2008 Spin Master LTD. & SEGA Toys 30/48

#9 BAKUGAN: Translucent Pyrus Dragonoid

A GREAT BRAWLER BECAUSE: Dragonoids are fan-favorite Bakugan (in part because the main character in the Bakugan story, Dan, is protected by a Guardian Dragonoid). This particular Pyrus Dragonoid is "hot" because it's made of a special material that makes it clear, or translucent, which makes it an even rarer find among the Bakugan Battle Brawlers!

CARD: Dragonoid

POWERFUL BECAUSE: Even dragons can use a boost now and then, and the Dragonoid card does just that! Many Dragonoids have good G Powers, so having your Dragonoid's G Power doubled is an awesome way to practically guarantee victory for yourself! *(Note that the card should read "get double their G Power," since Bakugan themselves don't actually have Holo Sector Point—HSP—values.)*

DAN'S DRAGONOID!

Dan has a Guardian Dragonoid, one associated with fire. Do you know what it's called?

A) Aquos Drago   B) Pyrus Drago   C) Darkus Drago

Answer: B) Dan's Dragonoid is called Pyrus Drago. The other types are Haos (light), Aquos (water), Sub Terra (earth), Ventus (wind), and Darkus (dark).

G WIZ!

What's a G Power? Easy—it's how strong your Bakugan is! It's written on the inside of your Bakugan. (Sometimes you might have to look hard to find the G Power on your Bakugan the first time—it might be covered up from when it was in the packaging!) The same Bakugan type can have lots of different G Powers, going even higher than 600 in some cases.

So, let's pretend you used Pyrus Dragonoid with a G Power of 450 to go to battle. You roll it onto the Dragonoid Character card you put into play, and when your opponent's Bakugan opens there, too, you have to figure out your G Power. Your Character card says that Dragonoids get their G Power doubled—so, your 450 is now 900. Then you add the benefit of the card for Pyrus Bakugan, another 150. So, your Pyrus Dragonoid has a final G Power of 1050. Will it be enough?

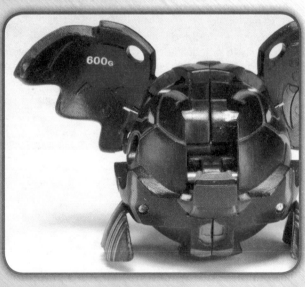

BAKUGAN: Aquos Juggernoid

A GREAT BRAWLER BECAUSE:
Juggernoids are seemingly unstoppable, in part because of their impressive armor. Many of the Juggernoids in Bakugan Battle Brawlers have good G Powers, and so they see a lot of action. One of the characters in the popular *Bakugan* TV show, Christopher, has a Guardian Aquos Juggernoid.

CARD: Black Hole

POWERFUL BECAUSE: Though you might not want to play this card with your Aquos Bakugan (since they get -200!), it's a great way to add a quick 100 to your final score at the end of the game. If you're close to winning but need just a few more points, play this card when you're down to your last Bakugan. If you win the battle, you end the game and still gain the 100 HSP for that Bakugan because of this card's special rule!

ANSWERING THE CALL

Want to get ready for the call to brawl? Booster Packs come with one Bakugan (and one metal card) in them, Starter Packs with three Bakugan and three cards, and Battle Packs come with an impressive six Bakugan and six metal cards! You'll be ready to battle instantly!

#7

BAKUGAN: Ventus Cycloid

A GREAT BRAWLER BECAUSE: The one-eyed Cycloids from the swift, silent space of Ventus are especially tough battlers—one of their kind, a Sub Terra, is the Guardian Bakugan to Billy Gilbert, one of the highest ranked Bakugan Brawlers in the world of the TV show. The Ventus Bakugan seem to have some of the highest G Powers in the game.

CARD: Battlefielder

POWERFUL BECAUSE: Play this card a little later in the game, when you have some idea what your opponent has been using for Gate cards. Then, when you use Battlefielder, you'll give yourself the advantage of controlling the battlefield by knowing exactly what's out there. Plus, you'll take HSP right out of your opponent's win pile!

BATTLEFIELDER

300
200
-150
-50
200
100

Winner takes one card from the loser's win pile and places it back on the battlefield.
Le vainqueur prend une carte capturée à un adversaire, et la remet sur le champ.

HSP 250

BAKUGAN ™ 2006 SPIN MASTER LTD. & SEGA TOYS   BA007-CO-SM-E

DVD TO VICTORY!

The *Bakugan Battle Brawlers* TV show, which began airing on the Cartoon Network® in February 2008, made its DVD debut in August 2008 with the first five episodes. Each DVD came with an exclusive trading card for the game, like Darkness to Victory, which can make your opponent play with his or her Gate cards face up! The second volume, "Game On," was released in late 2008.

BAKUSTORAGE!

Storing your Bakugan can be challenging—after all, they want to roll out for battle all the time. A BakuClip will store three of your Bakugan (and you can choose from all six colors). And a BakuRack will hold five BakuClips, letting you carry an impressive 15 Bakugan the next time you answer the call to brawl!

#6

BAKUGAN: Haos Tigrerra

A GREAT BRAWLER BECAUSE: Runo Misaki, the young girl who has long had a crush on Dan, has a Guardian Haos Tigrerra. The Haos Tigrerra (from the light space of Haos) is also among the most popular of this particular Bakugan because of its ferocious tigerlike look.

CARD: Point Slam

POWERFUL BECAUSE: If your opponent keeps coming up with those Bakugan with amazing G Powers, Point Slam will bring that to a halt! Of course, you have to be careful how you play this—with even a weak Haos Bakugan, Point Slam's boost of 250 will probably mean your own Bakugan will have its G Power reduced to 100 as well!

POINT SLAM

50

150

250

-250

-150

200

A battling Bakugan™ worth more than 400 G Power is reduced to 100. Un Bakugan™ qui livre bataille, valant plus de 400 points, n'en vaut plus que 100.

H S P 250

BAKUGAN ™ 2006 SPIN MASTER LTD. & SEGA TOYS.

DID YOU KNOW . . . ?

In the original TV show, Runo's Tigrerra was a male, but it was changed to a female for the English release.

#5 BAKUGAN: Special Attack Powered Up Evolution Aquos Dragonoid

A GREAT BRAWLER BECAUSE:
The Special Attack Powered Up Bakugan are among the most sought after by collectors because of their exceptionally high G Powers. Combine this quality with a Dragonoid type, and you have a Bakugan with a G Power over 500 that's hard to resist . . . and even harder to beat!

CARD: Peacemaker

POWERFUL BECAUSE: If you play this card carefully with your Aquos Bakugan, your opponent will be surprised to find that his or her brawling Bakugan has much less G Power than yours. If you combine this with another card like G-Power Bump to make it even stronger, your Bakugan is sure to win the battle. Plus, Peacemaker is sometimes worth as much as 300 HSP—that could help your final score a lot when the game is done!

BAKUGAN WEB BRAWLERS!

The official Bakugan Web site is your best source for Bakugan battles. It has all the information you want—what's new for the Bakugan Battle Brawlers game, an episode guide for the TV show, the characters and Bakugan that bring the battles to life, and even a great learn-to-play demo! Get your parent's permission before logging on to brawl!

#4 BAKUGAN: Pyrus Siege

A GREAT BRAWLER BECAUSE: Siege Bakugan are very aggressive with high G Powers, and the Pyrus Siege Bakugan are especially strong. But since the rules don't allow you to play with three Pyrus Siege Bakugan (you have to have three different colors of Bakugan), try using a Pyrus, an Aquos, and a Darkus Siege for your entire arsenal!

CARD: Match Points

POWERFUL BECAUSE: This is the Gate card that will reward you for playing with more than one Siege Bakugan in your arsenal. If you're a good shooter, you'll get to combine their G Powers. Notice that Pyrus, Aquos, and Darkus all get the highest boosts from this card—and that matches the three Siege Bakugan perfectly!

BUILDING YOUR BAKUGAN BATTLEGROUND

It's not always easy to find the perfect place to battle—unless you can take it with you! BakuMats are the fastest way to set up for you and three friends to do battle, and it comes with a convenient carrying case. You can also use the Bakugan Battle Arena, which gives you a hard, measured playing surface plus raised edges to keep your Bakugan from rolling too far from the battle!

#3

BAKUGAN: Darkus Tuskor

A GREAT BRAWLER BECAUSE: Players like the Darkus Bakugan because of how well they often do when supported by Ability or Command cards. Tuskor is an unusual-looking Bakugan, kind of like an elephant, which makes it even more interesting. But it's the G Power that gets the victory in battle, and Darkus Tuskor is one of the Bakugan with a G Power of 600 that players have had good luck finding!

CARD: HSP 400

POWERFUL BECAUSE: A Normal card that can make a huge difference for you at the end of the game when it's time to figure out the points and who won. This particular HSP Normal card comes with different boosts for different Bakugan, so choose one that helps your arsenal the best. More important, it will put an impressive 400 HSP in your win pile, which is amongst the highest HSP around!

HONORABLE MENTION: DUCK & WIN

Another great card to play against an opponent who keeps coming at you with high G-Powered Bakugan, Duck & Win is a little harder to use. Its boosts are so high for most Bakugan that you need to be sure to use it with only Aquos Bakugan or else you just might boost your own Bakugan to a defeat!

DUCK & WIN

110
60
90
120
140
110

The Bakugan with the lowest G-Power total wins this battle.

BA150-GA-SM Bakugan™ 2008 Spin Masters LTD. & SEGA Toys 18/48

#2

BAKUGAN: Ventus Manion

A GREAT BRAWLER BECAUSE: This sphinxlike Bakugan
has gained a reputation as being one of the most powerful
Bakugan in the game because
quite a few of them have
popped up recently with *MORE*
than 600 G Power. (The highest
G Power recorded so far is 630,
and that can still easily go up!)
The price of these when they're
sold individually can be quite
high, so your best bet to find
this powerful Bakugan is to
watch for it in Booster packs!

CARD: G-Power Exchange

POWERFUL BECAUSE: If
you want to take advantage
of an opponent who plays
with Bakugan that have
giant G Powers, cards like
Peacemaker (see #5) and
G-Power Exchange can
turn the game for you. Play
with Bakugan that have low
G Powers and dare your
opponent to brawl with
you when you're waiting to
make your own weakness
your strength.

The Bakugan have their printed G-Power swapped.

BA151-GA-SM Bakugan™ 2008 Spin Masters LTD. & SEGA Toys   19/48

LAUNCHING INTO ACTION

Some Brawlers use two fingers to press down on the edge of their Bakugan to set them back-spinning into battle. Others rocket their Bakugan forward with their thumbs, and still others flick them with one finger. However you get your Bakugan moving, there's another option—try the Bakugan Launcher. It comes with three ways of firing (curve shots, angle shots, and distance shots), and it even gives you a range meter to help you perfect your aim!

KNOW YOUR BAKUGAN!

Learn to tell a Skyress from a Storm Skyress and a Preyrs from a Preyrs II. It's easy when you have the cool promo poster available on the Bakugan Web site. Get your parent's permission to check out 48 different kinds of Bakugan so you'll know what you're up against the next time you head into the Bakugan Arena for a brawl!

#1

BAKUGAN: Translucent Haos Hynoid

A GREAT BRAWLER BECAUSE: Even with an average G Power of 400, this Bakugan is still so popular that it sometimes sells for more than a hundred dollars. Other Bakugan are more popular with players who know the TV show—the Darkus Hydranoid, for example, is the Bakugan of Masquerade, a very important character in the show. But the Haos Hynoid—and specifically, the translucent version of it—is extremely hot with collectors!

CARD: Doom Card

POWERFUL BECAUSE: In the TV show, the villain Masquerade has a Doom Card, a very powerful card that takes the opponent's Bakugan. So, some players have been worried that this card allows your opponent to take your Bakugan if you lose, but that's not the case—it's mixing up what happens on the show with what happens in the game. Instead, Doom Card simply removes the losing Bakugan so it can't come around again for the rest of the brawl between you and your opponent. A valuable, rare card to have when you've worked hard to beat one of your opponent's powerful Bakugan! This is easily the most expensive card in Bakugan Battle Brawlers, and once you have it work for you, you'll know why!

Written by Michael G. Ryan
Designed by Eric Medalle
Edited by Betsy H. Pringle
Product photography by Keith Megay
Production management by Larry Weiner

The Ultimate Guide to Trading Card Games is produced by becker&mayer!, LLC,11120 NE 33rd Place, Suite 101, Bellevue, WA 98004

www.beckermayer.com

If you have questions or comments about this product, please visit www.beckermayer.com/customerservice.html and click on the Customer Service Request Form.

✍ SCHOLASTIC

Scholastic Inc.
New York, NY
www.scholastic.com

Scholastic and associated logos are trademarks of Scholastic Inc.

ISBN-13: 978-1-60380-039-6

ISBN-10: 1-60380-039-5

Printed in the U.S.

10 9 8 7 6 5 4 3 2 1